JOURNEY TO WEALTH

The complete guide to credit repair

BRETT MITCHELL

authorHOUSE®

AuthorHouse™
1663 Liberty Drive
Bloomington, IN 47403
www.authorhouse.com
Phone: 1-800-839-8640

First published by AuthorHouse   6/2/2011

ISBN: 978-1-4634-0817-6 (sc)
ISBN: 978-1-4634-0818-3 (e)
ISBN: 978-1-4634-0816-9 (dj)

Library of Congress Control Number: 2011909515

Printed in the United States of America

Take Back Your Credit:

Remove Damaging Data from Your Credit History and Regain Control of Your Finances

Brett Mitchell

Limited Warranty and Disclaimer

This self-help book is intended to be used by consumers for their own benefit. It may not be reproduced in any way, resold, or used for commercial purposes without written permission from the publisher.

Information contained in this book was obtained from sources believed (but not guaranteed) to be reliable. The concepts presented herein represent the opinions of the author. You should obtain competent advice from your tax advisor or attorney before making any decisions based on this material.

I dedicate this book to my daughters Brittney and Ashley.
You both have given a joy and a love to me that words can never explain!
We have shared so much, you both have been my very best friends!
I love you both with all my heart, thank you!

CONTENTS

INTRODUCTION

Have you ever been turned down for credit because of derogatory information in your credit report? I have. It all started years ago, when I was a freshman in college. I was offered cards from several major credit card companies. I applied for and received three cards with credit limits between $500 and $3,000. I was amazed that these companies extended credit to me; it was like free money (so I thought).

At the time, I was working as a seasonal holiday employee for a department store. I purchased Christmas gifts for family and friends using my new credit cards. Not long afterward, I was laid off from my part-time job and had no other income. I was current on my credit card payments up until the layoff. Within months, I maxed out my credit cards using the lines of credit to pay other bills. This strategy for making ends meet was indeed the beginning of my financial downfall.

As an unemployed student, I was overwhelmed by my credit card debt. When I was unable to make my payments, my accounts were sent to collection agencies. For months, I received collection notices and phone calls every day. I thought if I ignored the phone calls and letters from the collection companies, my problems would disappear; how wrong I was! The calls did stop after about a year, with an occasional collection letter here and there. I believed that I had fallen off their radar. I thought that all was well. Wrong again.

A few years later, I got married. Life was great! We were renting an apartment and wanted to purchase a home for our growing family. After shopping around, my wife and I found the perfect home. I went to my bank and applied for a mortgage with them, but I was denied due to derogatory information in my credit report. I applied with a few banks and was denied by all but one, which required me to have a cosigner. I was unable to get a cosigner, derailing my dream of being a homeowner. To add insult to injury, the collection companies started to actively pursue me again. Collection companies are alerted whenever you apply for credit or a loan. Credit reporting agencies give collection companies your updated financial information: new address, employer, phone number, and so on.

A few months later, I tried to re-establish my credit by paying off my old credit card debts. I repaid my creditors, believing that by doing so, I would establish good credit again. Soon after repaying all my debts, I applied for a credit card with a department store but was denied. After I received the denial letter, I ordered a copy of my consumer credit report. To my dismay, even though I had paid off the collection accounts from my old college days, the negative information from those accounts was still on my report. Paying those creditors was not the great fix that I thought it would be. In fact, paying off my collection accounts without negotiating favorable terms with my creditors did more harm than good. The collection accounts were now showing as paid, but the account was still a negative element on my report. When potential creditors view your credit report and see any collection account, paid or unpaid, they view that as derogatory. After paying hundreds of dollars to settle these collection accounts, I found myself in an even worse place financially. I was out hundreds of dollars, and my negative credit remained the same. I was unable to get a retail credit card due to my bad credit. This was the moment that convinced me to find a cure for my situation.

After years of attending seminars and workshops and consulting with attorneys and financial experts, I learned what I needed to do to restore my credit. I read every book that I could find on consumer credit and credit repair. I discovered loopholes in the laws that govern consumer credit and protect the consumer. I learned about debt validation, which I call the Ultimate Secret Weapon, which you can use to remove negative information from your credit report, and it is all legal. If you apply these techniques to your situation, you can see amazing results in weeks. I have outlined the blueprint to rehabilitating your credit in these rough economic times. If you learn the methods in this book, your credit problems will be a thing of the past.

After you repair your own credit, you can charge others a fee for performing that service for them. Some credit consultants earn over $100,000 a year restoring people's credit. There is a strong market for these services in today's harsh economic times. Even as a part-time business, you can earn hundreds of dollars a month; all you need is the time to read and learn these methods and have faith in yourself.

The information in this book can change your life and increase your prosperity. Knowledge is power, but only when used properly. Remember, you don't have to be a victim of the system; you can make the system work for you. Here is how!

Chapter One:

What are credit Bureaus, Credit Reports, and Credit Scores?

It is very important to have good credit in the United States today, because it can help enhance your quality of life. Many nice things you may want to buy must be financed or bought on credit. Credit reporting is a multibillion-dollar industry. According to ACA International, a trade association of credit bureaus and mortgage reporting companies, there are about 12,000 credit reporting agencies (CRAs) in the United States. There are three national credit reporting agencies: Experian, Equifax, and Trans Union. Credit reporting agencies are not part of any government agency. They are independent businesses.

Experian, formerly known as TRW, is one of the "Big Three" credit reporting bureaus. Experian is headquartered in Dublin, Ireland. Equifax, formerly known as Retail Credit Company, was founded in 1899 and is headquartered in Atlanta. Trans Union was founded in 1968.

CRAs store information on every American who applies for or uses credit. Every time you apply for a credit card or a loan with a bank, the lender checks your credit rating with one or more of these credit reporting agencies. Companies that subscribe to these credit agencies use the information contained in your file to determine your creditworthiness. They believe that how you repaid other creditors in the past is a good indication of how you will pay your debts in the future.

To report information to a credit agency, a creditor must be approved for membership. Banks, finance companies, retail stores, landlords, and real estate management companies subscribe to the credit agencies for their services. Once a creditor subscribes for the services, they can access information from your credit history, which the CRA stores in a database. That information includes your age, address (present and past), employment history, and bill payment patterns.

CRAs also search public records for bankruptcy information, judgments, and tax liens from federal, local, and state courts. Bankruptcies are usually updated on a daily basis. Courthouse data collections are updated weekly or monthly. CRAs are regulated by the US Fair Credit Reporting Act (FCRA) of 1971. The act was updated and amended in 1997 and 2003. The Federal Trade Commission (FTC) is responsible for enforcing the FCRA, which protects consumers against inaccuracies on their credit report. The FCRA details the proper procedures to use if a creditor reports inaccurate information about you. The letters in Appendix A are tailored to force creditors and collection companies to remove any incorrect data from your credit report. Appendix B presents the act for your information.

What Is a Credit Report?

Your *credit report* is a record of your past borrowing and repaying habits, including information about late payments and bankruptcy. The term *credit reputation* is synonymous with *credit history* or *credit score.* Your credit report is simply a detailed account of your credit history. The report will contain creation information, such as current credit accounts, payment history, credit usage, and other information from public records.

In the United States, when you fill out an application for credit from a bank, store, or credit card company, your information is forwarded to a credit bureau. The credit bureau matches your name, address, and other identifying information with information in its files. That's why it is very important for creditors, lenders, and others to provide accurate data to credit bureaus.

This information is used by lenders, such as credit card companies, to determine your creditworthiness—your willingness to repay a debt. This is indicated by how timely your past payments to other lenders have been. Lenders like to see consumer debt obligations paid on a consistent, timely basis.

There has been much discussion over the accuracy of the data in consumer credit reports. However, scientific studies using sample sizes large enough to be valid have concluded that, by and large, the data in credit reports is very accurate. The credit bureaus point to their own study of 52 million credit reports to highlight that their data is very accurate. The Consumer Data Industry Association testified before Congress that less than 2 percent of those reports that resulted in a consumer dispute required data to be deleted because it was in error. When you dispute information in your credit report, the credit bureau has thirty days to verify the data. Over 70 percent of these consumer disputes are resolved within fourteen days. According to the Federal Trade Commission, one credit bureau claimed that 95 percent of those who disputed an item were satisfied with the outcome

The other factor used by lenders to determine whether they will provide you with credit or a loan is your income. The higher your income, all other things being equal, the more credit you can access. However, lenders make credit-granting decisions based on both ability to repay a debt (your income) and willingness as indicated by the past payment history (your credit report).

These factors help lenders determine whether to extend credit and on what terms. With the adoption of risk-based pricing on almost all lending in the financial services industry, this report has become even more important since it is usually the sole element used to set the annual percentage rate (APR), grace period, and other contractual obligations of the credit card or loan.

What Exactly Is a Credit Score?

In the world of lending, there is nothing more important than your credit score. The three-digit score determines whether banks or financial institutions will extend you credit or allow you to borrow money for a home. Your credit score is a representation of your creditworthiness.

Credit scores and credit reports are two different things, although the credit score ultimately depends on your credit report.

Credit scores range from 300 to 850. This score is also referred to as your FICO score Your credit score takes into account a lot of different information from your credit report, but it's not all treated equally; some aspects of your credit history are more important than others, making them count more toward your overall score. Your FICO score is made up of five items: payment history (35%), total amount owed (30%), length of credit history (15%), new credit: (10%), and type of secured or unsecured credit in use (10%).

The majority of your credit score comes from your payment history and how much debt you have. These two items account for 65 percent of your credit score. Keep this in mind if you are looking to improve your score; you need to address these issues first

Why Your Credit Score Is Important

Why is your credit score so important? It will follow you for the rest of your life. When you try to borrow money, the lender will look at your credit score to decide whether you are creditworthy or not. Need to buy a car? Looking for a home mortgage? They will check your credit score. Looking for a job? Today, some employers check credit scores to determine if an applicant is reliable or not

Improving Your Credit Score

So you made some mistakes in the past and now your credit score is low? Don't worry; your credit score is updated every month, as you make improvements to your credit history. Keep in mind that negative items will stay on your report for seven years (a little longer for certain bankruptcies, which remain for ten years). Don't let that worry you; this book presents an aggressive (and totally legal) method to improve your credit history and score.

Chapter Two:

How Do You Rate And How To Repair Your Credit

Negative credit information (such as late payments, collection accounts, judgments, and tax liens) can deter a lender from issuing you credit or a loan, regardless of your ability to repay. There are three types of information in a credit report: positive, neutral, and negative. The following items are consider positive:

- Paid as agreed

- Paid satisfactorily

- Current with no late payments

- Account closed by consumer's request

Neutral statements involve negative remarks that are under investigation, lost credit cards, and so on. The following statements are considered negative:

- Payment late thirty days, sixty days, etc.

- Paid or unpaid charge-offs

- Paid or unpaid collection accounts

- Bankruptcy Chapter 7 or Chapter 13

- Judgments

- Accounts closed at grantor's request

- Tax liens

Most Americans have at least one derogatory remark in their credit file. In some cases, these negative remarks are wrong and misleading. These errors can be caused by clerical mistakes, mistaken identity, or fraud. You may find that an account that has been current is now considered negative. You may find someone else's information on your report. This happens a lot with people who have common names or juniors and seniors who reside at the same household.

In light of the financial crisis that led to the current economic recession, many people are unable to make ends meet. Unemployment, health care problems, and other setbacks have caused many Americans to fall behind on their bills. Unfortunately, these setbacks may continue to trouble them for years to come in terms of negative credit. Poor judgment is the major cause of negative credit. Many people overextend themselves with credit cards, loans, auto loans, and second mortgages. With poor management, they often found themselves in financial trouble, burdened with high debts.

Many people today are faced with economic problems. Things can really seem dim when you are burdened with bills you cannot pay. Just remember that you are not alone; more than 26 percent of American adults, 58 million people, have bad credit. That is according to statistics from the website creditcards.com.

If you are rejected for credit, take action to restore your credit. If you want to repair your credit or re-establish your credit, regardless of your situation, the first thing you need to do is get a copy of your credit report.

All Americans are entitled to free credit report from each of the three major credit reporting agencies: Experian, Equifax, and Trans Union. These credit reporting agencies are required to provide each consumer, upon request, a free copy of their credit report, once every twelve months. These reports are not sent automatically. You can request these reports by visiting AnnualCreditReport.com, which is the only authorized online source for consumers to retrieve their annual credit report for free. You can receive the Annual Credit Report request brochure by calling the Federal Trade Commission at (877) 332-8228. You can complete the form on the brochure and mail it to Annual Credit Report Request Services, PO Box 105281, Atlanta, GA 30348-5281.

Here are some steps to take to raise your credit score:

(1) **Pay Down Your Credit Cards:** Paying off an installment loan, mortgage, auto loan, or student loan can help your score, but not as much as paying down or paying off a revolving credit account. Lenders like to see large gaps between the amount of credit you're using and your available credit limits. If you keep your balance below 30 percent of your credit limit, it can really improve your score. While most experts recommend paying off the card with the highest rate first, a better strategy is to pay down the cards that are closest to their limits.

(2) **Use Your Credit Cards Wisely:** Racking up big balances can hurt your score, even if you pay your bill in full each month. What is reported to the credit agencies and calculated into your scored are the balances reported on your last statements. (Not that paying off your balances each month isn't financially smart, it's just that the credit agencies do not care.) You should keep your balance below 30 percent of your card's limit.

(3) **Check Your Limits:** Your score might be lowered if your lender shows a lower limit than you actually have.

(4) **Use Old Cards:** The older the credit history, the better. If you stop using your oldest cards, the lender may stop updating the accounts at the credit bureaus. The account will still appear, but it won't have as much effect on the credit scoring formula as your active accounts. You should use your old credit cards every few months to keep them active; charge small amounts and pay it off in full when the statement arrives.

(5) **Dispute Negative Items:** Disputing erroneous negative items can greatly improve your credit score. Look for and correct errors such as late payments, charge-offs, collection accounts that are not yours, credit limits reported lower than they actually are, accounts listed as "Settled," paid derogatory accounts, and negative information older than seven years (ten years for bankruptcy).

Now that you have a copy of your credit report, you are ready to repair your credit. Next, you need to know your legal rights. The Fair Credit Reporting Act (FCRA), 15 USC Section 1681 A through 1681 T, protects consumers against erroneous credit information that results in an unfair description of your credit rating or worthiness (see Appendix B). According to the FCRA, you have the following rights:

Right 1. You are allowed to challenge the accuracy of your credit report at any time.

Right 2. The credit agencies must reinvestigate anything you challenge.

Right 3. The credit bureau must reinvestigate the disputed information within thirty days (this time period begins when the bureau receives notice of your dispute). The only exception to the thirty-day rule is when you send the bureau additional items within the period. The bureau may extend the deadline a maximum of fifteen days.

Right 4. If the credit bureau cannot confirm the information you have challenged within a reasonable time period, it must delete the information from your credit files.

Right 5. If a creditor verifies the information and the credit bureau responds in a timely manner, the negative marks will remain on your records. You have the right to submit a consumer statement of your views of the situation.

Start Repairing Your Own Credit

First, understand the following rules:

(1) Don't make hasty decisions.

(2) Don't be scared; you are not the only one with this problem.

(3) Don't believe anything a credit agency says to you; always get

it in writing.

(4) You do not owe money until a judge or jury says you do.

(5) Be organized.

(6) Use Google to search for updates on new credit laws.

(7) Be patient; this process does not happen overnight.

(8) Never speak to anyone on the phone who is attempting to collect on a debt, *period*! You preserve your rights legally when all communication is done by writing.

(9) Never include your Social Security number with any letter to a collection company.

(10) If you get a fancy letter in the mail with a law firm's logo stamped on it, don't worry. Collection agencies often use fancy letterheads to bring out your worst fears.

Where Do You Start?

(1) Get Organized

A. Buy four three-ring binders and label them "Experian," "Equifax," "Trans Union," and "Collection Letters." On your computer, create a folder for each of the binders.

B. Buy thirty packs of three-ring divider inserts.

C. Go to the post office and grab a stack of forty green return cards and green return receipt forms. (It is easier to fill these out at home ahead of time.)

D. Buy a box of envelopes with tear-off glue strips.

E. Buy a stapler.

F. Buy a couple of different colored highlighters and pens.

G. Buy a stamp that says "Received" and has a place to write the date.

H. Buy one or two yellow legal pads.

I. Buy a box of manila folders or an expandable accordion file holder (the kind you sort bills with).

K. Buy a plastic bin or storage box to hold your binders and supplies.

(2) Get Informed

Review your credit reports from Experian, Equifax, and Trans Union.

(A) Read your credit reports. Read them again, and then reread them.

(B) Learn what the laws are in your state regarding statute of limitations (SOL).

(3) Keep Records

A. Insert each credit report into its appropriate three-ring binder. Stamp the credit report with your "Received" stamp and write the date on it. Use a divider insert to separate it from the next one.

B. Go through your credit reports and highlight the creditors that are problems.

C. Start organizing your old statements by putting them in chronological order, up to the last statement you made a payment on. Put the statements in the accordion file.

D. Do the same with your bank statements, checks, and so on.

E. Make a chart with three columns; write down each creditor in the first column. Write the date you made your last payment in the second column, and write the SOL date in the final column. SOL dates can be a little tricky. For example, let's say your state's SOL is three years and your last payment was January 1, 2003. Well, technically on January 1, 2006, your

SOL would be up. However, some courts have been known to allow credit agencies and original creditors up to an extra 180 days. So adjust according to what your local courts allow.

Make three copies of this form; put a copy on the front of each binder. This will make a handy reference and reminder. If any of your collections are past the SOL, congratulations! You can delete them. Always challenge any negative listing and aim to completely delete it. When you challenge information within a charge-off or court records, it may not be enough to remove the negative listing. The credit bureau may just update the negative information, which would keep the account as negative. When disputing accounts, such as bankruptcies, foreclosures, repossessions, court judgments, collection accounts, charge-offs accounts, and settled accounts, it's best to use "Not my account" or "Never late" for late accounts (more than thirty days late).

Always dispute everything on your credit report that is not correct: current and previous employers, addresses, and maiden names. Make sure that the credit bureaus show only one entry for each of the following: your legal name (no extra nicknames or maiden names), your current address, and your Social Security number.

Dispute each incorrect item individually, not all at once. This will keep the credit reporting agency from claiming that your request for an investigation is frivolous. You can, however, challenge several items in one letter, but you must give separate and complete instructions for each item.

Write a letter to each credit reporting bureau listing the negative items you want deleted. Your letter should clearly state the item you are disputing and why you're disputing it. Always provide a reason for your dispute (for example, "Not late," "Never late," "Not mine").

It is your right to dispute a negative item even if you were late paying on the account, as long as you have reason to believe that the account is inaccurate, unverifiable, or obsolete. Always include any documentation that substantiates your dispute, such as a creditor's letter stating that the information is false.

F. Make a copy of the letter.

G. Fill out your green card and return receipt form and head over to the post office. Mail the letter and keep the receipt. Always send all mail certified with return receipt; this confirms the date that your letter was received.

H. Staple the receipt to your copy of the letter and insert it into the proper binder. Documenting your progress can mean the difference between failure and success in cleaning up your credit report. This documentation is necessary if you decide to sue your creditors.

I. Debt validation is an important step if you have lots of collection accounts on your credit report. This is one of the best ways to legally have a collection account deleted from your credit report. Under the Fair Debt Collection Practice Act (FDCPA), you have thirty days to dispute the debt and question its validity. However, even if the thirty days has passed, the collection agency is unlikely to have proof that you received the collection letter from them. In reality, you can request debt validation from the collection company at any time. Debt validation will be discussed in chapter 4.

J. Now your next step is to sort out all of your collection accounts within your credit report. Send letters to each collection agency. As always, fill out your green postal cards and keep copies and receipts for each letter. Insert them in the appropriate three-ring binder. Always use divider tabs to keep your papers organized.

K. In about seven to ten days, you will start receiving green cards in the mail. Take the green card and staple it to the copy of the letter alongside the mailing receipt.

L. In about forty-five days, you will start to receive responses to the letters you sent out. The ones that come from the credit reporting agencies will have a copy of your latest credit report and notations on what was done, verified, deleted, and so on. Make sure you stamp these with your "Received" stamp and mark the date you received them. Insert the credit report into the appropriate file folder.

The first forty-five days are the most important. Make sure you review your three-ring binders every week. This way, you can confirm whether you are getting information returned to you in the legal time frame required (this will be important for follow-up letters).

Having everything in chronological order at your fingertips lets you keep track of reaged accounts or accounts inserted after debt has passed the SOL. Do not take the initial collection letters sent to you lightly. You must respond to them within thirty days to protect your rights.

Credit bureaus are engulfed with customer credit issues during certain holidays, such as Christmas and New Year's. The credit bureaus receive millions of credit applications and requests to check consumers' credit during this time, and many of their employees are absent due to vacation or sick time. Take this into consideration. This makes it extremely hard for the credit bureaus, creditors, and collection companies to investigate and resolve credit disputes. The absenteeism, high volume of work, and lack of staff work in your favor. There are more negative trade line or negative account deletions during the months of November through January than in any other months.

Chapter Three:

How To Appeal Credit Card Rejection And Win

Appealing rejections is one of the most important parts of credit improvement. Most of the credit applications I submitted while rebuilding my credit were rejected. I appealed each of these rejections and was ultimately approved in most cases.

The first step in appealing a rejection is to find out why the rejection occurred. If the rejection letter does not state the reason, contact the lender and find out why you were rejected and what can be done about it. Get the name and title of the person you can appeal to.

Write this person a polite but firm letter, disputing the reasons for the rejection by presenting facts in a new light or offering new information. Attach any relevant documentation. Tell the creditor why you represent a good credit risk. Reassure the creditor that your account will translate into consistent profits over the years to come.

Remember, lenders make money by extending you credit. They want your business. It makes sense to appeal; a good lender is never upset by an appeal. When Citi-bank decreased my line of credit from $2,500 to $500, I sent them a credit appeal letter like the one in Appendix A. After they investigated and upheld my appeal, they sent me a letter informing me that my credit had been restored.

CHAPTER FOUR:

OUR METHODS TO RAISE YOUR SCORE

Piggyback Method

The Piggyback method is a great way to increase your credit score. It works by adding you to someone else's credit trade line account. Credit card applications include a section to add a cardholder. If the owner of the account adds you to their account, then their payment history shows up on your credit report as well. Therefore, you should only pursue this method with someone who has perfect credit. The account owner must have held the account for at least five years with a perfect payment history. The account owner must also have a balance of only 30 percent of the credit limit.

The account owner can call the credit card company and request to add you as a joint cardholder. Once you are added, the entire account information and history becomes your information as well. By adding three to seven trade lines in this matter, you can increase your credit score seventy-five to one hundred points.

It may not be easy to find someone who is willing to add you to their trade line account, especially if you have bad credit. Your parents and other family members may also decline because they do not want you to damage their good credit. There are broker companies that sell trade line accounts. The company connects you with a person with a perfect trade line and sells you their account trade line for profit. The account owner adds you as a joint user, but you do not get a card, PIN, or information that pertains to the account. The account information and bills are only sent to the account owner. Nevertheless, as a joint user, you will still benefit with a higher score.

Due to the potential for abuse, the Piggyback method has come under close scrutiny. Regulators were said to be considering abolishing the procedure, but as of 2011, the Piggyback method of credit score building was still in effect. However, be aware that credit is being examined thoroughly. Most credit underwriters will only add joint users to a credit card who reside in the same household as the account holder.

Consumer Credit Counseling

Consumer credit counseling services are designed to assist people who have large amounts of debt. However, many consumer counseling programs offer no real solution for their clients.

Consumer credit counselors assess your overall financial condition. They take your monthly liabilities, assets, and expenses into account and set up a payment program for you. They contact your creditors to propose a payment schedule so that you can pay off your debt. When they reach an agreement with a creditor, you make a monthly payment to the consumer credit counseling company. The monthly payment includes a maintenance fee (usually fifteen to thirty dollars) for the credit counseling company, which also charges a setup fee.

Many credit counseling companies claim to be nonprofit, but you must be careful to avoid signing up with an unscrupulous company. Credit counseling companies are not regulated by the federal government, and only a few states have restrictions on them.

Some credit counseling companies have been accused of not dispersing their clients' funds to the creditors on time, in result, damaging their credit further. If they arrange for you to make payments that are lower than the minimum, you will incur late charges, which will show up on your credit report. Credit counseling has more negatives than positives, so be careful when selecting an agency to assist you. When the risks are weighed, you may determine that there is no reward in using a credit counseling company. Your best option is to make payment agreements directly with your creditors; ask them to lower your APR or consolidate your debt into one account. You may be surprised at how many lenders will work with you in these rough economic times.

Debt Validation: The Ultimate Secret Weapon

One important aspect of the Fair Debt Collection Practices Act is the section regarding debt validation (see Appendix C for the complete text of the act). As a protection to consumers who are in dispute with debt collectors, the federal government allows consumers to challenge the validity of any debt claimed by a collection agency. Validation of debt is discussed in Section 809 of the act, which states the following:

(a) Within five days after the initial communication with a consumer in connection with the collection of any debt, a debt collector shall, unless the following information is contained in the initial communication or the consumer has paid the debt, send the consumer a written notice containing:

(1) The amount of the debt;

(2) The name of the creditor to whom the debt is owed;

(3) A statement that unless the consumer, within thirty days after receipt of the notice, disputes the validity of the debt, or any portion thereof, the debt will be assumed to be valid by the debt collector;

(4) A statement that if the consumer notifies the debt collector in writing within the thirty-day period that the debt, or any portion thereof, is disputed, the debt collector will obtain verification of the debt or a copy of a judgment against the consumer and a copy of such verification or judgment will be mailed to the consumer by the debt collector; and

(5) A statement that, upon the consumer's written request within the thirty-day period, the debt collector will provide the

consumer with the name and address of the original creditor, if different from the current creditor.

(b) If the consumer notifies the debt collector in writing within the thirty-day period described in subsection (a) that the debt, or any portion thereof, is disputed, or that the consumer requests the name and address of the original creditor, the debt collector shall cease collection of the debt, or any disputed portion thereof, until the debt collector obtains verification of the debt or any copy of a judgment, or the name and address of the original creditor, and a copy of such verification or judgment, or name and address of the original creditor, is mailed to the consumer by the debt collector.

What all this means in plain English is that if you write a letter to the collection agency disputing their claim within thirty days of receiving their initial letter, they must show you written proof that you owe the aforementioned debt(s). To make the proof legitimate, they must include the following:

- A copy of the original credit card application or financing agreement that you signed

- Account statements from the original creditor

- Proof that said collection agency has been assigned to the debt

At the same time, send a letter to the credit bureaus disputing the information involving the collection account. If the collection agency fails to write back within thirty days, send another letter to the credit bureaus stating that the collection agency did not respond to your request for debt validation and thus has not complied with the FDCPA (even if the credit bureau has sent you a letter saying the debt is verified). The credit bureaus should remove the collection account(s) at this time.

If they don't cooperate, you may have to write a new letter threatening a lawsuit for willful noncompliance. Of course, you don't want to take it that far, especially if it's not a large amount. But this is one way to stave off the debt collectors and potentially solve a big problem with a little bit of legwork.

You may be out of luck if the collection agency is diligent and sends you the information in a timely fashion. If they validate the debt, you have few options other than to pay the debt or risk a charge-off or a lawsuit. Either way, set aside a folder with all the original documents you use to state your case. Be careful how you approach both the debt collectors and the credit bureaus, and if you aren't familiar with the law, it may be wise to seek legal help before pursuing a lawsuit.

Credit Inquiries and Your Credit Score

A credit inquiry appears on your credit report when you apply for some type of consumer credit loan (credit cards, auto loans, mortgage, etc.). These inquiries will appear in your credit report whether you are issued the credit or not. The main purpose for reporting an inquiry to the credit reporting agencies is to let other creditors know that you are trying to open a new line of credit.

Appling for credit too many times within a certain time frame can damage your credit score, so do not apply for credit too often.

A credit inquiry can stay on your credit report for up to two years. An inquiry that affects your credit score is called a "Hard Pull." This type of inquiry is established when you apply for a credit card, auto loan, or mortgage. An inquiry that was not initiated by you for loan purposes is called a "Soft Pull." These are the inquiries that you pull on yourself (for your consumer credit report) or that a potential employer may pull on you.

While inquiries are important, your credit score, payment history, and account balances carry more weight. Do not worry that much about Soft Pulls. Too many Hard Pulls, however, may make creditors view you as being desperate.

Debt Collection Statute of Limitations

Statute of limitations, when dealing with credit issues, is a legal term that places restrictions on how long a creditor can file a lawsuit for delinquent debt. Once the time has expired for the debt collection, creditors can no longer enforce their collections through the courts. This eliminates the customer obligation in repaying the debt. If the creditor tries to sue you, you can use the expired SOL as a legal defense.

Bill collectors may still call and harass you, but there is no legal method that they can use to collect payment from you. The statute of limitations starts from the date of the first delinquency and ends with the time lines posted in your state laws.

Rapid Rescoring

Rapid rescoring is a method mortgage companies use to quickly update their account information; consumers can use this method to increase their credit scores in a short period of time. Rapid rescoring increases your credit score by reflecting accounts that have been paid in full, accounts with lower balances, and deleted negative information.

By rapid rescoring negative accounts, you can raise your credit score a great deal within weeks. It is possible to see your score increase thirty-five to fifty points in five to seven days. If you are going to make a major purchase like buying a home, then rapid rescoring will help bring your score up. Discuss the benefits with your mortgage broker to determine if it is right for you.

CHAPTER FIVE

BANKRUPTCY, CREDIT CARDS, AND COLLEGE STUDENTS

What Is Bankruptcy?

Bankruptcy is a remedy when a person or business is unable to pay their outstanding debts. A federal judge evaluates the circumstances and either discharges the debt or sets up a payment schedule.

There are three kinds of bankruptcies: Chapter Seven, Chapter Thirteen, and Chapter Eleven. The two chapters that we are most concerned with are Chapters Seven and Chapter Thirteen. This book does not discuss Chapter Eleven, which is typically used for business bankruptcies.

Bankruptcy laws help give individuals with unmanageable debt the chance for a fresh start by discharging their debts. There are some debts that are not discharged: criminal fines, student loans, child and spousal support, and taxes.

Chapter Seven Bankruptcy

Chapter Seven bankruptcy begins when the debtor files a petition with the bankruptcy court. The debtor must release an exact list of assets and liabilities along with the petition. The debtor also has to release all nonexempt property to the bankruptcy trustee, who will deliver these assets to the creditors.

A husband and wife may file a joint petition or individual petitions. If the debtor's income is less than 150 percent of the poverty level, and the debtor is unable to pay the Chapter Seven fees, even in installments; the courts may waive the requirement to pay these fees.

Chapter Seven bankruptcy will eliminate unsecured debts, such as credit card debt, medical bills, and other debts. Individuals who file a Chapter Seven can keep secured debts, such as a home mortgage, auto payments, and furniture payments.

Chapter Seven will stop bill collectors from calling. Chapter Seven will also stop garnishments and most civil judgments. Once a creditor receives notice that you have filed bankruptcy, all collection efforts must stop. If a creditor still uses collection methods after being legally informed of your bankruptcy, the creditor may be liable for damages.

Chapter Thirteen Bankruptcy

With Chapter Thirteen bankruptcy, the court works out a plan to pay off the debts over a period of time. These cases are designed for individuals who have regular income. The bankruptcy court supervises a repayment plan that allows the debtor to reorganize their debts. A Chapter Thirteen plan will prevent your home from being foreclosed and your vehicle from being repossessed. A Chapter Thirteen plan may also provide for the payment of certain debts that cannot be discharged in a Chapter Seven bankruptcy, such as student loans and taxes.

The size of the monthly payments are determined by assessing the individual's living expenses. Typical Chapter Thirteen plans last for no more than five years. This may vary based on income and the amount of debt owed.

Which Bankruptcy Is Right for You?

With Chapter Seven bankruptcy, all of your eligible debts are wiped away at once. You may have to sell off your assets. Chapter Seven is called the "Liquidation Bankruptcy"; it is a fresh start. However, child support debt, student loans, and taxes are not eligible to be discharged under Chapter Seven.

With Chapter Thirteen, all of your debts are consolidated into one monthly payment. Under Chapter Thirteen bankruptcy, the debtor remains under court supervision for the life of the plan, up to sixty months. The debtor cannot make new debts or sell assets without the permission of the courts. The payment plan can be deducted directly from the debtor's paycheck by court order.

Chapter Seven bankruptcy remains on your credit report for up to ten years. However, Chapter Thirteen bankruptcy remains on your credit report for only seven years.

The Bankruptcy Abuse Prevention and Consumer Protection Act of 2005 requires that a debtor receive credit counseling from an approved agency before filing bankruptcy. After filing a bankruptcy case, and before debts are discharged, a debtor must receive financial education from an approved agency.

Credit Cards and College Students

When students graduate from college, they get more than just a degree. Many college graduates obtain credit cards while they are in school, and if they do not use them responsibly, they will incur credit card debt. Now this does not mean that college students should cut their credit cards up, it just means that when they use them, they need to do so responsibly. They need to realize that a credit card comes with responsibility, and when the responsibility is not met, it can lead to the biggest mistake of their life. Good credit provides more benefits today than ever; good credit in today's society is financially mandatory.

Once you graduate from college, you will find out that having a good credit score is the key to obtaining a car loan, signing a lease for an apartment, being offered a good job, or getting a mortgage (especially one with a good interest rate). Today, car insurance companies check credit scores to determine what rate to charge you.

Obtaining a credit card is an excellent way to build your credit score. Making your monthly payments on time and keeping your balance at less than 30 percent of your limit shows creditors you are creditworthy.

When making a decision on which credit card to apply for, compare the following important features:

- Annual percentage rate (APR). This is the charge on the balance that you do not pay off. If you pay the total amount due each month, then the APR is not important, but you can compare different cards by checking their APR. Some credit cards have a low rate (or a zero rate) for a short period of time; check to see what the interest rate will be once the teaser rates expires.

- Credit limit. Your credit limit is the maximum amount you can charge on the credit card. Having a higher credit limit increases your credit score, but if you have a history of overspending, choose a credit card with a lower limit.

- Grace period. Some credit cards offer a grace period before interest charges are incurred. The best advice is to apply for a credit card that offers a grace period. The interest charge only applies if you do not pay off the full balance.

- Fees. Most credit card companies charge late fees, and some charge a fee if you go over your limit. Some credit cards also charge an annual fee and application fee. It is best to avoid these fees, but if you are new to credit, you may not have a choice. After you use your card responsibly for a year or two, you may be able to have the annual fee eliminated or reduced.

If you are under twenty-one years old, you must be able to show the credit card company that you can pay the monthly balance. Another way to receive a credit card is by having someone with good credit cosign for you.

What should you do once the card is in your hand? Credit cards are great to have, but only if they are used responsibly. Using a credit card irresponsibly can hurt your credit score and cost you more money. Before using your credit card to make a purchase, always ask yourself if the purchase is affordable and necessary. If you charge more than you can pay monthly, it will lead to higher payments and increased interest costs.

Most people do not earn much money on their first job after graduation, so make sure you factor in your student loan payments when you set up your budget. Wait to apply for a credit card until you are making enough to pay that debt in addition to your other living expenses.

Once you get a credit card, be sure to make your monthly payment on time. If you make your payments late each month, your credit score will be damaged, you may incur a higher APR, and you could be charged late fees. Set up a schedule to make your credit card payment on the same date each month. Many credit card companies give you the option of paying your bill on-line, which removes the worries of forgotten payments or payments being lost in the mail. If you pay by mail, make sure you send your payment ahead of time so the creditor receives your payment before the due date. This way you can avoid late fees or charges for paying the bill over the phone.

Graduating from college, stepping out on your own, and becoming an adult is incredibly exciting. Don't let your new life be ruined because of credit card debt. Use your credit cards responsibly, develop good spending habits, and guard your credit score with your life. Having a good score can mean the difference between having a good life and just getting by.

Imagine getting a certified letter in the mail, notifying you of a court order judgment against you from ABC Credit Corp. You ask yourself, how did this happen? How did this judgment come about without your knowledge of it? Let us take a close look at the events that took place.

About three years ago, you opened an account with ABC Credit Corp. for a credit card. ABC Credit Corp issued you a credit card with a $5,000 limit. For the first two years, you paid your account on time until you had an unsuspected hardship that maxed out your card limit. Over the next year, due to your hardship, you were unable to make the monthly payments on your account, so ABC placed the account in its credit department for review. Over the next 120 days, ABC's credit department tried contacting you by phone and mail, but was unable to reach you. ABC Credit Corp assigned your account to a collection agency. The collection agency proceeded with their efforts against you, with notice after notice. You never responded to the letters or phone call from the collection agency. The collection agency eventually took out a summons against you for what you owe to them. The court sent you a notice to answer the summons, but you ignored the letter. The case reached civil court, and by default, the judge issued a judgment against you for not answering the summons. Now you receive a notice by mail that you owe $5,000 plus other additional fees for court costs, lawyer fees, and so on.

Definitions:

1. **A judgment is a court decision that was entered in favor of the person suing.**

2. **Motion to vacate means if you were sued and lost because you did not appear in court, you can file a notice of motion to vacate judgment. You are asking**

the court to delete the judgment against you and give you a new hearing.

3. **Plaintiff is the person who brings an action in a court of law.**

4. **Defendant is the person being sued.**

How can a judgment be overturned?

Filing a motion to dismiss a judgment is similar to filing an appeal. You should file a motion to dismiss a judgment if the outcome was unfair or you have a good reason as to why the court should overturn its prior decision.

There are many collection agencies that attempt to place judgments in court that do not follow the law. Most judges overseeing these cases do not specialize in this sort of law. A judge ruling in a small claims case may not fully understand consumer law. Most judges understand the basics, but no one judge can know all aspects of the law. Most judges have to research state statutes and case decisions before ruling on a case. If the plaintiff claims that he or she followed the procedures correctly and you do not dispute this, the judge most likely will give the plaintiff the benefit of the doubt.

There are two main reasons that a judgment is granted to the plaintiff:

1. When the defendant failed to respond to the court summons with the proper paperwork within the allowed time period.

2. When the defendant failed to appear for their court date. This is called winning by default. If you miss your court date and had good reason for not appearing for the hearing and the court agrees with you, then you may be able to get the judgment vacated.

How to prepare your motion to vacate:

1. Study your state's court procedures before making your

motion to vacate. First look at your state's rules of civil procedure. It will show you exactly how you should file your motion. It will also tell you what reasons are valid in getting your judgment dismissed within your state. Failure to follow proper procedures may get your motion dismissed on a technicality. The court only responds to violations of existing laws. The court will not accept excuses such as, "My insurance company was supposed to pay this debt and never did, therefore I do not have to pay this bill."

2. File the proper paperwork! Your motion to vacate should be filed in the same court that granted the judgment against you. Advise the court clerk with your typed document that you are filing a motion to vacate a judgment. You may need additional forms to prepare, along with the court filing fees. The court clerk would know exactly what needs to be done with your legal papers.

3. The court will notify you and the original plaintiff of the new court date. The original plaintiff will have thirty days to respond (depending on your state's rules regarding court procedures) to your motion to vacate. Very often the original plaintiff in your lawsuit will offer to vacate the judgment when the following occurs:

   A. When the original plaintiff does not have the proper documentation that you were served.

   B. When the original plaintiff is unable to prove that the debt was legal to collect in the first place.

   C. When the original plaintiff is unable to show what the correct amount of the debt should be.

   D. When the original plaintiff is unable to show the original signed contract.

   E. When the debt is outside your state's statute of limitations.

You should be well prepared and have records of all documents available on your court case present at your hearing. If you win, the court will send you a document showing the case was dismissed. You should send copies to the credit bureaus to remove any and all negative trade lines associated with this account. Keep these documents for your records, along with any other court records from your case.

Owning a home is sometimes described as the American dream, and it may be a dream you share. Homes can provide a sense of belonging and become the center of family traditions. Owning your home can also be a smart move financially, since you are buying a valuable asset with the money you spend for shelter. Someday you may be able to make a profit by selling your home for more than you paid to purchase it.

Few people have enough money on hand to cover the full cost of buying a home. Most pay a portion with money they have saved and finance the rest with a mortgage or long-term loan.

The more you know about what mortgages cost and how to qualify for one, the more comfortable you will be about moving forward on buying a home.

Renting vs. Buying?

If you are looking for a new home, your first decision is whether to buy or rent. Like many people, the emotional satisfaction of being a homeowner is an excellent feeling. The financial reward of being a homeowner is very rewarding as well. Buying a home is a big commitment, and you want to be sure you are ready to make that decision.

Renting and buying each have some drawbacks. When you rent, you do not build equity, and your rent may increase when you renew your lease. When you buy, you have to expect increasing insurance and tax bills plus the regular cost of keeping your home in good condition.

What Can You Afford?

If you decide to buy, you must ask the crucial question, what can I afford? You have to ask yourself if you have enough cash saved for a down payment, which is usually 3 to 20 percent of the total cost of the home. For example, if the purchase price is $100,000, you will need $10,000 for a 10 percent down payment.

First-time home buyers can check with their local bank or lending institutions for programs designed to help them. This may include down payment assistance, closing cost assistance, lower rates, and educational programs.

Finding a Mortgage

Financial companies such as banks, savings and loans, credit unions, and mortgage lenders compete with each other for your business; it is wise to shop around and compare rates and fees.

Preapproval means that you submitted an application and the lender qualified you to receive a mortgage before you even choose a home. If the lender approves you, you are guaranteed to borrow up to a specific amount. This allows you to enter the home buying market knowing exactly how much you have to spend. Another advantage of being preapproved for a mortgage is that sellers maybe more likely to accept your bid for their home if you can guarantee you have a mortgage. That is because sales contracts are often contingent on the buyer's ability to borrow and can fall through if a mortgage application is not approved.

Closing on Your House and Loan

Once you have chosen a home to buy, you need to have a home appraisal done, along with a title search on the property you are purchasing. The final step in buying your new home is called the closing settlement. Before the closing, you will receive a good faith estimate in writing from the lender listing the settlement costs you can expect to pay at the closing (usually 2 to 10 percent of your loan).

The day you close, the parties involved in the transaction will meet. This can include the home buyer, the seller, their attorneys, and so on. The buyer will write numerous checks for the balance of the selling price and the closing costs, including the following:

1. Title searches and title insurance to protect the lender and you against any potential legal claims to the property

2. Attorney's fees

3. Property taxes to reimburse the seller for amounts that have already been paid

4. Transfer taxes

5. Prepayment of property taxes and homeowners insurance to the lender, so that money is available to pay these bills as they come due.

In conclusion, I would like to stress that the best way to gain good credit is to pay what you owe and pay it on time. You have to realize that the companies and individuals that extended credit to you believed in your ability to repay them. Your responsibility is to confirm that trust by repaying what you owe.

Good credit is an instrument that you can use to help improve the quality of life for you and your family. Good credit can increase your standard of living as well; it can be used to finance your education, purchase a home, make investments, and much more.

Never take your credit for granted; it is almost impossible to navigate within our financial times without the use of credit. This book is a good start to in helping you get on course to achieving good credit. It is my desire that you absorb the information within this book and apply it to your own situation. Please feel free to write me and share your testimonials. Good luck in all your endeavors, and may you live long and proper!

APPENDIX A

LETTERS TO REMOVE INACCURATE CREDIT INFORMATION

[Recipient Name]

[Recipient Address]

[Recipient City, State Postal Code]

[Account Item List]

[Date]

[Recipient Name],

I am writing to advise you that you are inaccurately reporting information to the credit agencies regarding the above account. You are in violation of the Fair Credit Reporting Act, section 623 Responsibilities of Furnishers of Information. The FTC defines your obligations at: www.ftc.gov/bcp/conline/pubs/buspubs/infopro.htm

I hereby dispute your information in its entirety and request supporting documentation that substantiates the information you have furnished to the credit agencies.

Please be advised that I am not requesting a verification that you have my mailing address. Rather, I am requesting validation, i.e., competent evidence that I had some contractual obligation sans consumer protection encumbrance which incurred the original claims associated with this trade line.

Should you not be able or willing to provide me with the substantiating documentation as verification to cure this violation, within the next 30 days, please have the information **DELETED** from each of the CRAs to whom you initially furnished it.

Continued unsubstantiated reporting of possible inaccuracies to third parties may provide a basis for civil complaints being filed in accordance with the FCRA, and other federal statutes. If this matter remains unresolved, I will have no recourse but to consider legal action as a resolution.

[Your First Name] [Your Last Name]

[Your Address]

[Your City, State Postal Code]

Follow-Up Failed to Provide Validation (Aggressive Response)

[Recipient Name]

[Recipient Address]

[Recipient City, State Postal Code]

[Date]

Dear Sir/Madam:

I have not heard back from you in over 30 days regarding my registered notice of dispute of [Account Item List]. You have also not supplied the demanded proof of the alleged debt. Your continued silence is unacceptable.

For the record, I state again that since I have no account with you, nor am I your customer, nor have I entered into a contract with you, I must ask that you return to me copies of the following information in addition to the form provided at the end of this letter:

- **Agreement with your client that grants you the authority to collect on this alleged debt.**

- **Copies of all notices of repossession, proof of legal delivery of said notices.**

- **Full accounting of the proceeds of repossession sale, and proof of sale being held in a commercially reasonable manner.**

- **Account history including beginning balance, every payment received and date it was posted to the account, any fees charged to the account, interest and interest rate charged to the account, along with any other account information you may have available.**

- **Agreement that bears the signature of the alleged debtor agreeing to pay the creditor.**

- **Any insurance claims which have been made by any creditor regarding this account**

- **Any judgments which have been obtained by any creditor regarding this account**

You have fifteen (15) days from receipt of this notice to respond. Your failure to respond in a timely manner will work as a waiver to any and all of your claims in this matter, and will entitle me to presume that you sent your letter(s) in error. If in fact this error has been made, remove the trade line from my credit files and this matter will be permanently closed.

Failure to respond within 15 days of receipt of this registered letter or failure to remove the incorrect information from my credit reports will force me to consider legal action in a small claims action against your company. I will be seeking damages for the following violations of the FDCPA:

Unfair practices (www.ftc.gov/os/statutes/fdcpa/fdcpact.htm#808)

False or misleading representation (www.ftc.gov/os/statutes/fdcpa/fdcpact.htm#807)

I will be seeking damages for the following violation of the FCRA: because you state that you are responsible for how the trade line is being reported to the credit reporting agencies, you are also in violation of § 623. Responsibilities of furnishers of information to consumer reporting agencies [15 USC § 1681s-2] (www.ftc.gov/os/statutes/fcra.htm#623).

For the purposes of 15 USC 1692 et seq., this Notice has the same effect as a dispute to the validity of the alleged debt and a dispute to the validity of your claims. This Notice is an attempt to correct your records, and any information received from you will be collected as evidence should any further action be necessary. This is a request for information only, and is not a statement, election, or waiver of status.

I affirm under penalty of perjury under the laws of the United States of America, that the foregoing is true and correct, to the best of my knowledge and belief.

Sincerely,

[Your First Name] [Your Last Name]

[Your Address]

[Your City, State Postal Code]

Cc: Attorney General

Debt Validation Form Questionnaire for [Account Item List]

Original Creditor's Name:

Name of Debtor:

Address of Debtor:

Balance of Account:

Date you acquired this debt:

This Debt was: assigned -or- purchased

Please indicate any credit bureaus to which you have reported negative marks:

Experian _____

Equifax _____

Trans Union _____

Follow-Up Failed to Provide Validation

[Recipient Name]

[Recipient Address]

[Recipient City, State Postal Code]

[Your First Name] [Your Last Name]

[Your Address]

[Your City, State Postal Code]

[Date]

Validate: [Account Item List]

Your firm has failed to send the legally required validation of this debt. You have been notified that your actions are detrimental to me and that your firm has violated the law (including but not limited to the Consumer Credit Protection Act, the Fair Credit Reporting Act, and the Fair Debt Collection Practices Act).

Your firm knew or should have known that the actions taken against me and the information collected about me was inappropriate and damaging to me.

You have failed to use reasonable care in the course of business and failed to use even minimal procedures to ensure that I was not harmed.

You have communicated and are continuing to communicate incorrect and defamatory information to third parties, including, but not limited to, Equifax, Experian, and Trans Union.

As a result of these blatantly reckless, wanton, and intentional acts, I have suffered and continue to suffer general and specific damages. I am also very upset at your firm's intentional infliction of emotional distress and at the other diminishments of the quality of my life.

I am now demanding the immediate and complete removal of this trade line from my credit reports (Equifax, Experian, and Trans Union).

As I am currently attempting to apply for credit, time is of the essence. Please understand that I am extremely concerned about the consequences of the actions your firm is having on my life. Please be advised that, if this matter is not resolved in 30 days, I will take any and all necessary steps to protect my rights.

Thank you in advance for your attention to this matter.

Sincerely,

[Your First Name] [Your Last Name]

Sample Round 1 Letter

[Your First Name] [Your Last Name]

[Your Address]

[Your City, State Postal Code]

[Recipient Name]

[Recipient Address]

[Recipient City, State Postal Code]

Date

Dear Sir or Madam:

I am writing for two (2) reasons:

1. To dispute certain information in my credit file; and

2. To have you investigate/reinvestigate and remove inaccurate information from my credit report and prevent its reinsertion. The item(s) I dispute are listed below and are inaccurate or incomplete. I am requesting that the item be investigated to correct the information.

Below are the items:

[Account Item List]

Please reinvestigate this (these) matter(s), and delete or correct the disputed items within the time frame required by the Fair Credit Reporting Act (FCRA) and inform me in writing of the outcome. Thank you for your time and consideration in this matter.

Sincerely,

[Your First Name] [Your Last Name]

[Your SSN]

BRETT MITCHELL

[Your DOB]

[Your Address]

[Your City, State Postal Code]

Sample Round 1. Request For Deletion

[Recipient Name]

[Recipient Address]

[Recipient City, State Postal Code]

[Date]

This letter is a formal complaint that you are reporting inaccurate credit information. I am very distressed that you have included the below information in my credit profile due to its damaging effects on my good credit standing. As you are no doubt aware, credit reporting laws ensure that bureaus report only accurate credit information. No doubt the inclusion of this inaccurate information is a mistake on either your or the reporting creditor's part.

Because of the mistakes on my credit report, I have been wrongfully denied credit recently, which was highly embarrassing and has negatively impacted my lifestyle. The following information therefore needs to be verified and deleted from the report as soon as possible:

[Account Item List]

Please delete the above information as quickly as possible.

Sincerely,

[Your First Name] [Your Last Name]

[Your SSN]

[Your DOB]

[Your Address]

[Your City, State Postal Code]

Follow-Up Verification Procedure

[Recipient Name]

[Recipient Address]

[Recipient City, State Postal Code]

[Date]

RE: Formal Request for Verification Procedures

FCRA § 611. Procedure in case of disputed accuracy [15 USC § 1681i]

To Whom It May Concern:

I received notice that you verified certain trade lines on my credit report from the following companies:

[Account Item List]

Please tell me how you did that. Who did you talk to at the original credit grantor? Did you write them? Was a UDF form used or was this through electronic automatic dispute verification? Did you contact them at the same address/phone number listed on my report? The FCRA says that you have to tell me this in 15 days if I ask. Don't provide the generic response of how you use various methods. Tell me exactly how you verified them and include the full name of the person you spoke with.

Also, what is the date of the commencement of delinquency? The original creditor is required to give that to you. So when is that? And when will this trade line be past the reporting time frame? Don't provide the generic "7 years" response; I am aware of that. Tell me **specifically** when these accounts allegedly became delinquent, and **specifically** when they will be removed. Some of these accounts are reporting as charged off as well as being included in bankruptcy. So, which is it?

Supply your response within 15 days or delete the trade lines.

Regards,

[Your First Name] [Your Last Name]

[Your SSN]

[Your DOB]

[Your Address]

[Your City, State Postal Code]

Inquiry Dispute—Unauthorized

[Recipient Name]

[Recipient Address]

[Recipient City, State Postal Code]

[Date]

To Whom It May Concern:

The following "hard" inquiries were not authorized by me. Please delete them. Since I have never given permission for them to inquire about my credit status, they are unauthorized by me. Their continued presence on my credit report constitutes inaccurate information, which under the Fair Credit Reporting Act must be removed.

[Account Item List]

Furthermore, I would appreciate the names, addresses, and phone numbers of these companies so I may follow up.

Sincerely,

[Your First Name] [Your Last Name]

[Your SSN]

[Your DOB]

[Your Address]

[Your City State Postal Code]

Follow-Up—No Response, FTC Complaint

[Recipient Name]

[Recipient Address]

[Recipient City, State Postal Code]

[Date]

Dear Sir or Madam:

I sent your company a reinvestigation request regarding certain inaccurate items on my credit report. A copy of my original request is enclosed as an attachment.

In accordance with the Fair Credit Reporting Act, 15 USC section 1681i, your company is required to complete this reinvestigation within 30 days of receipt of my original request. This 30-day period has now passed, and I have not received any response from your company.

I believe that your company has been unable to verify the inaccurate information contained in my report, which is why I have not yet received a response. Please immediately remove the listed inaccurate items from my credit report.

Also, please send a corrected report to me and to anyone else who has requested a copy of my credit file within the last six months. I am sending a copy of this letter and the enclosed attachments to the Federal Trade Commission.

Sincerely,

[Your First Name] [Your Last Name]

[Your SSN]

[Your DOB]

Brett Mitchell

[Your Address]

[Your City, State Postal Code]

cc: Federal Trade Commission

Consumer Response Center

600 Pennsylvania Ave, NW

Washington, DC 20580

Demand Deletion After Validation with CA

[Recipient Name]

[Recipient Address]

[Recipient City, State Postal Code]

[Your First Name] [Your Last Name]

[Your SSN]

[Your DOB]

[Your Address]

[Your City, State Postal Code]

[Date]

Dear [Recipient Name]:

This is a request for deletion of a disputed item. I have attempted to have this alleged debt verified by the alleged creditor and collection agency to no avail. I am respectfully requesting the collection agency do what is legally mandated by the FCRA and FDCPA, and delete the following account listing:

[Account Item List]

I previously sent a demand for validation and they have failed to provide any proof or respond in any way. I sent a second letter. Again, I have received no response. I sent yet another letter. Again, I received no response. The FDCPA states that collection activity must cease until they have produced verification of the alleged debt if so requested.

As per the FTC, this includes reporting to the credit bureaus, which they obviously have done illegally. It is quite evident that no such proof of this alleged debt exists or they would have provided it in the previous months since it was requested. Also, when an alleged debt is disputed, a notation must be entered on the debtor's report showing the item as in dispute. Again, this was not done. Another violation of the FDCPA.

As per the FCRA, if no proof of debt exists, it may not be reported to the credit reporting bureaus. The FCRA also states that the credit reporting agencies must accept written proof from the debtor. Therefore, I am not asking for an investigation to be done. I am requesting that the entry be deleted in its entirety since there is no proof of its existence.

Sincerely,

[Your First Name] [Your Last Name]

Dispute After Collection Agency

[Date]

Dear [Recipient Name],

I recently attempted to contact [Account Item List] on my credit report at the address listed on my the credit report. The letter was returned to me undeliverable because the company has "moved, left no address, return to sender, unknown forwarding address."

As you are well aware, under 15 USC § 1681i of the FCRA, as well as numerous other legal authorities, you are required by federal law to report only accurate information. You have violated my civil rights by repeatedly reporting inaccurate information when I request my credit report, and when lenders view my report. This is a violation of federal law that provides me with the right to seek remedy through the courts since it has caused me damage in how I am viewed by lenders, and the terms of loans received and offered. I demand that within five days of receipt of this letter that the negative trade line associated with this complaint be deleted from my file, as required by the FCRA. If this demand is not met, I will be filing grievances with the Attorney General and the Federal Trade Commission. I look forward to an expedient conclusion to this issue.

Sincerely,

[Your First Name] [Your Last Name]

[Your SSN]

[Your Address]

[Your City, State Postal Code]

First name Last name

1212 Stone Drive

City, State 39191

Juniper Bank

PO Box 8828

Wilmington, DE 19899

May 11, 2005

Re: (Acct #xxxxxx)

Dear Customer Service:

Thank you for your prompt response to my Bank Card application. According to your disclosure statement dated 3/04/2005 (attached herewith), you were obliged to decline my request due to unpaid charge-off, public records, and collection items on my Trans Union report.

I am appealing to you to reconsider my application for the following reasons:

1. None of the negative items you stated are on my Trans Union report. I have perfect credit and never had an unpaid debt or one in collection.

2. I have ample credit references which include major financial institutions going back more than ten years.

3. In more than ten years of dealings with financial institutions, I have never made a single late payment, much less committed any serious transgression, such as defaulting on a loan or the like. In fact when I have been out of the country for any length of time, I have made payments in advance to insure against the possibility of any delinquencies. This fact is also verifiable and evidenced from my Trans Union Credit report, a copy of which I am attaching here.

I submit that a person who maintains a spotless credit record from the time he was a teenager until the age of 40 represents an excellent credit risk.

4. All financial institutions I have had loans or lines of credit with have always made money as a result because I access my line of credit and pay it back with interest. I never need to be reminded to make payments, so the bank saves on postage and various other administrative costs.

5. As far as my standing in the community is concerned, in addition to my position as president of my housing subdivision, I am also a member of Mt. Olive Baptist Church.

6. Here is a sampling of my credit references dating back quite a few years:

I have a paid-off $176,100 FHA Mortgage dating from 04/93 to 02/00; I was never late with any payment.

I have a paid-off $20,508 auto loan with GE Custom auto opened on 11/93 and paid on 05/97; I was never late with any payment.

Thank you for taking time out of your busy schedule to reconsider my application in light of the above information and attached documentation.

Sincerely,

First name Last name

Appendix B
Fair Credit Reporting Act

THE FAIR CREDIT REPORTING ACT

As a public service, the staff of the Federal Trade Commission (FTC) has prepared the following complete text of the Fair Credit Reporting Act (FCRA), 15 U.S.C. § 1681 et seq.

Although staff generally followed the format of the U.S. Code as published by the Government Printing Office, the format of this text does differ in minor ways from the Code (and from West's U.S. Code Annotated). For example, this version uses FCRA section numbers (§§ 601-625) in the headings. (The relevant U.S. Code citation is included with each section heading and each reference to the FCRA in the text.) Although the staff has made every effort to transcribe the statutory material accurately, this compendium is intended only as a convenience for the public and not a substitute for the text in the U. S. Code. This document was posted on July 30, 2004.

This version of the FCRA includes the amendments to the FCRA set forth in the Consumer Credit Reporting Reform Act of 1996 (Public Law 104-208, the Omnibus Consolidated Appropriations Act for Fiscal Year 1997, Title II, Subtitle D, Chapter 1), Section 311 of the Intelligence Authorization for Fiscal Year 1998 (Public Law 105-107), the Consumer Reporting Employment Clarification Act of 1998 (Public Law 105-347), Section 506 of the Gramm-Leach-Bliley Act (Public Law 106-102), Sections 358(g) and 505(c) of the Uniting and Strengthening America by Providing Appropriate Tools Required to Intercept and

Obstruct Terrorism Act of 2001 (USA PATRIOT Act) (Public Law 107-56), and the Fair and Accurate Credit Transactions Act of 2003 (FACT Act) (Public Law 108-159).

The provisions added to the FCRA by the FACT Act will become effective at different times.

In some cases, the provision includes its own effective date. In other cases, the FACT Act provides that the effective dates be prescribed by the FTC and Federal Reserve Board. See 16 CFR Part 602. (69 Fed. Reg. 6526; February 11, 2004) (69 Fed. Reg. 29061; May 20, 2004).

TABLE OF CONTENTS

§ 613 Public record information for employment purposes

§ 614 Restrictions on investigative consumer reports

§ 615 Requirements on users of consumer reports

§ 616 Civil liability for willful noncompliance

§ 617 Civil liability for negligent noncompliance

§ 618 Jurisdiction of courts; limitation of actions

§ 619 Obtaining information under false pretenses

§ 620 Unauthorized disclosures by officers or employees

§ 621 Administrative enforcement

§ 622 Information on overdue child support obligations

§ 623 Responsibilities of furnishers of information to consumer reporting agencies

§ 624 Affiliate sharing

§ 625 Relation to state laws

§ 626 Disclosures to FBI for counterintelligence purposes

§ 627 Disclosures to governmental agencies for counterterrorism purposes

§ 628 Disposal of records

§ 629 Corporate and technological circumvention prohibited

§ 601. Short title

This title may be cited as the "Fair Credit Reporting Act."

§ 602. Congressional findings and statement of purpose [15 U.S.C. § 1681]

(a) *Accuracy and fairness of credit reporting.* The Congress makes the following findings:

(1) The banking system is dependent upon fair and accurate credit reporting.

Inaccurate credit reports directly impair the efficiency of the banking system, and unfair credit reporting methods undermine the public confidence which is essential to the continued functioning of the banking system.

(2) An elaborate mechanism has been developed for investigating and evaluating the credit worthiness, credit standing, credit capacity, character, and general reputation of consumers.

(3) Consumer reporting agencies have assumed a vital role in assembling and evaluating consumer credit and other information on consumers.

(4) There is a need to insure that consumer reporting agencies exercise their grave responsibilities with fairness, impartiality, and a respect for the consumer's right to privacy.

(b) *Reasonable procedures.* It is the purpose of this title to require that consumer reporting agencies adopt reasonable procedures for meeting the needs of commerce for consumer credit, personnel, insurance, and other information in a manner which is fair and equitable to the consumer, with regard to the confidentiality, accuracy, relevancy, and proper utilization of such information in accordance with the requirements of this title.

§ 603. Definitions; rules of construction [15 U.S.C. § 1681a]

(a) Definitions and rules of construction set forth in this section are applicable for the purposes of this title.

(b) The term "person" means any individual, partnership, corporation, trust, estate, cooperative, association, government or governmental subdivision or agency, or other entity.

(c) The term "consumer" means an individual.

(d) Consumer Report

(1) *In general.* The term "consumer report" means any written, oral, or other communication of any information by a consumer reporting agency bearing on a consumer's credit worthiness, credit standing, credit capacity, character, general reputation, personal characteristics, or mode of living which is used or expected to be used or collected in whole or in part for the purpose of serving as a factor in establishing the consumer's eligibility for

(A) credit or insurance to be used primarily for personal, family, or household purposes;

(B) employment purposes; or

(C) any other purpose authorized under section 604 [§ 1681b].

(2) *Exclusions.* Except as provided in paragraph (3), the term "consumer report" does not include

(A) subject to section 624, any

(i) report containing information solely as to transactions or experiences between the consumer and the person making the report;

(ii) communication of that information among persons related by common ownership or affiliated by corporate control; or

(iii) communication of other information among persons related by common ownership or affiliated by corporate control, if it is clearly and conspicuously disclosed to the consumer that the information may be communicated among such persons and the consumer is given the opportunity, before the time that the information is initially communicated, to direct that such information not be communicated among such persons;

(B) any authorization or approval of a specific extension of credit directly or indirectly by the issuer of a credit card or similar device;

(C) any report in which a person who has been requested by a third party to make a specific extension of credit directly or indirectly to a consumer conveys his or her decision with respect to such request, if the third party advises the consumer of the name and address of the person to whom the request was made, and such person makes the disclosures to the consumer required under section 615 [§ 1681m]; or

(D) a communication described in subsection (o) or (x).

(3) *Restriction on sharing of medical information.* Except for information or any communication of information disclosed as provided in section 604(g)(3), the exclusions in paragraph (2) shall not apply with respect to information disclosed to any person related by common ownership or affiliated by corporate control, if the information is--

(A) medical information;

(B) an individualized list or description based on the payment transactions of the consumer for medical products or services; or

(C) an aggregate list of identified consumers based on payment transactions for medical products or services.

(e) The term "investigative consumer report" means a consumer report or portion thereof in which information on a consumer's character, general reputation, personal characteristics, or mode of living is obtained through personal interviews with neighbors, friends, or associates of the consumer reported on or with others with whom he is acquainted or who may have knowledge concerning any such items of information. However, such information shall not include specific factual information on a consumer's credit record obtained directly from a creditor of the consumer or from a consumer reporting agency when such information was obtained directly from a creditor of the consumer or from the consumer.

(f) The term "consumer reporting agency" means any person which, for monetary fees, dues, or on a cooperative nonprofit basis, regularly engages in whole or in part in the practice of assembling or evaluating consumer credit information or other information on consumers for the purpose of furnishing consumer reports to third parties, and which uses any means or facility of interstate commerce for the purpose of preparing or furnishing consumer reports.

(g) The term "file," when used in connection with information on any consumer, means all of the information on that consumer recorded and retained by a consumer reporting agency regardless of how the information is stored.

(h) The term "employment purposes" when used in connection with a consumer report means a report used for the purpose of evaluating a consumer for employment, promotion, reassignment or retention as an employee.

(i) The term "medical information" --

(1) means information or data, whether oral or recorded, in any form or medium, created by or derived from a health care provider or the consumer, that relates to--

(A) the past, present, or future physical, mental, or behavioral health or condition of an individual;

(B) the provision of health care to an individual; or

(C) the payment for the provision of health care to an individual.

(2) does not include the age or gender of a consumer, demographic information about the consumer, including a consumer's residence address or e-mail address, or any other information about a consumer that does not relate to the physical, mental, or behavioral health or condition of a consumer, including the existence or value of any insurance policy.

(j) Definitions Relating to Child Support Obligations

(1) The "overdue support" has the meaning given to such term in section 666(e) of title 42 [Social Security Act, 42 U.S.C. § 666(e)].

(2) The term "State or local child support enforcement agency" means a State or local agency which administers a State or local program for establishing and enforcing child support obligations.

(k) Adverse Action

(1) *Actions included.* The term "adverse action"

(A) has the same meaning as in section 701(d)(6) of the Equal Credit Opportunity Act; and

(B) means

(i) a denial or cancellation of, an increase in any charge for, or a reduction or other adverse or unfavorable change in the terms of coverage or amount of, any insurance, existing or applied for, in connection with the underwriting of insurance;

(ii) a denial of employment or any other decision for employment purposes that adversely affects any current or prospective employee;

(iii) a denial or cancellation of, an increase in any charge for, or any other adverse or unfavorable change in the terms of, any license or benefit described in section 604(a)(3)(D) [§ 1681b]; and

(iv) an action taken or determination that is

(I) made in connection with an application that was made by, or a transaction that was initiated by, any consumer, or in connection with a review of an account under section 604(a)(3)(F)(ii)[§ 1681b]; and

(II) adverse to the interests of the consumer.

(2) *Applicable findings, decisions, commentary, and orders.* For purposes of any determination of whether an action is an adverse action under paragraph (1)(A), all appropriate final findings, decisions, commentary, and orders issued under section 701(d)(6) of the Equal Credit Opportunity Act by the Board of Governors of the Federal Reserve System or any court shall apply.

(l) The term "firm offer of credit or insurance" means any offer of credit or insurance to a consumer that will be honored if the consumer is determined, based on information in a consumer report on the consumer, to meet the specific criteria used to select the consumer for the offer, except that the offer may be further conditioned on one or more of the following:

(1) The consumer being determined, based on information in the consumer's application for the credit or insurance, to meet specific

criteria bearing on credit worthiness or insurability, as applicable, that are established

(A) before selection of the consumer for the offer; and

(B) for the purpose of determining whether to extend credit or insurance pursuant to the offer.

(2) Verification

(A) that the consumer continues to meet the specific criteria used to select the consumer for the offer, by using information in a consumer report on the consumer, information in the consumer's application for the credit or insurance, or other information bearing on the credit worthiness or insurability of the consumer; or

(B) of the information in the consumer's application for the credit or insurance, to determine that the consumer meets the specific criteria bearing on credit worthiness or insurability.

(3) The consumer furnishing any collateral that is a requirement for the extension of the credit or insurance that was

(A) established before selection of the consumer for the offer of credit or insurance; and

(B) disclosed to the consumer in the offer of credit or insurance.

(m) The term "credit or insurance transaction that is not initiated by the consumer" does not include the use of a consumer report by a person with which the consumer has an account or insurance policy, for purposes of

(1) reviewing the account or insurance policy; or

(2) collecting the account.

(n) The term "State" means any State, the Commonwealth of Puerto Rico, the District of Columbia, and any territory or possession of the United States.

(o) *Excluded communications.* A communication is described in this subsection if it is a communication

(1) that, but for subsection (d)(2)(D), would be an investigative consumer report;

(2) that is made to a prospective employer for the purpose of

(A) procuring an employee for the employer; or

(B) procuring an opportunity for a natural person to work for the employer;

(3) that is made by a person who regularly performs such procurement;

(4) that is not used by any person for any purpose other than a purpose described in subparagraph (A) or (B) of paragraph (2); and

(5) with respect to which

(A) the consumer who is the subject of the communication

(i) consents orally or in writing to the nature and scope of the communication, before the collection of any information for the purpose of making the communication;

(ii) consents orally or in writing to the making of the communication to a prospective employer, before the making of the communication; and

(iii) in the case of consent under clause (i) or (ii) given orally, is provided written confirmation of that consent by the person making the communication, not later than 3 business days after the receipt of the consent by that person;

(B) the person who makes the communication does not, for the purpose of making the communication, make any inquiry that if made by a prospective employer of the consumer who is the subject of the communication would violate any applicable Federal or State equal employment opportunity law or regulation; and

(C) the person who makes the communication

(i) discloses in writing to the consumer who is the subject of the communication, not later than 5 business days after receiving any request from the consumer for such disclosure, the nature and substance of all information in the consumer's file at the time of the request, except that the sources of any information that is acquired solely for use in making the communication and is actually used for no other purpose, need not be disclosed other than under appropriate discovery procedures in any court of competent jurisdiction in which an action is brought; and

(ii) notifies the consumer who is the subject of the communication, in writing, of the consumer's right to request the information described in clause (i).

(p) The term "consumer reporting agency that compiles and maintains files on consumers on a nationwide basis" means a consumer reporting agency that regularly engages in the practice of assembling or evaluating, and maintaining, for the purpose of furnishing consumer reports to third parties bearing on a consumer's credit worthiness, credit standing, or credit capacity, each of the following regarding consumers residing nationwide:

(1) Public record information.

(2) Credit account information from persons who furnish that information regularly and in the ordinary course of business.

(q) Definitions relating to fraud alerts.

(1) The term "active duty military consumer" means a consumer in military service who--

(A) is on active duty (as defined in section 101(d)(1) of title 10, United States Code) or is a reservist performing duty under a call or order to active duty under a provision of law referred to in section 101(a)(13) of title 10,

United States Code; and

(B) is assigned to service away from the usual duty station of the consumer.

(2) The terms "fraud alert" and "active duty alert" mean a statement in the file of a consumer that--

(A) notifies all prospective users of a consumer report relating to the consumer that the consumer may be a victim of fraud, including identity theft, or is an active duty military consumer, as applicable; and

(B) is presented in a manner that facilitates a clear and conspicuous view of the statement described in subparagraph (A) by any person requesting such consumer report.

(3) The term "identity theft" means a fraud committed using the identifying information of another person, subject to such further definition as the Commission may prescribe, by regulation.

(4) The term "identity theft report" has the meaning given that term by rule of the Commission, and means, at a minimum, a report--

(A) that alleges an identity theft;

(B) that is a copy of an official, valid report filed by a consumer with an appropriate Federal, State, or local law enforcement agency, including the United States Postal Inspection Service, or such other government agency deemed appropriate by the Commission; and

(C) the filing of which subjects the person filing the report to criminal penalties relating to the filing of false information if, in fact, the information in the report is false.

(5) The term "new credit plan" means a new account under an open end credit plan (as defined in section 103(i) of the Truth in Lending Act) or a new credit transaction not under an open end credit plan.

(r) Credit and Debit Related Terms

(1) The term "card issuer" means--

(A) a credit card issuer, in the case of a credit card; and

(B) a debit card issuer, in the case of a debit card.

(2) The term "credit card" has the same meaning as in section 103 of the Truth in Lending Act.

(3) The term "debit card" means any card issued by a financial institution to a consumer for use in initiating an electronic fund transfer from the account of the consumer at such financial institution, for the purpose of transferring money between accounts or obtaining money, property, labor, or services.

(4) The terms "account" and "electronic fund transfer" have the same meanings as in section 903 of the Electronic Fund Transfer Act.

(5) The terms "credit" and "creditor" have the same meanings as in section 702 of the Equal Credit Opportunity Act.

(s) The term "Federal banking agency" has the same meaning as in section 3 of the Federal Deposit Insurance Act.

(t) The term "financial institution" means a State or National bank, a State or Federal savings and loan association, a mutual savings bank, a State or Federal credit union, or any other person that, directly or indirectly, holds a transaction account (as defined in section 19(b) of the Federal Reserve Act) belonging to a consumer.

(u) The term "reseller" means a consumer reporting agency that--

(1) assembles and merges information contained in the database of another consumer reporting agency or multiple consumer reporting agencies concerning any consumer for purposes of furnishing such information to any third party, to the extent of such activities; and

(2) does not maintain a database of the assembled or merged information from which new consumer reports are produced.

(v) The term "Commission" means the Federal Trade Commission.

(w) The term "nationwide specialty consumer reporting agency" means a consumer reporting agency that compiles and maintains files on consumers on a nationwide basis relating to--

(1) medical records or payments;

(2) residential or tenant history;

(3) check writing history;

(4) employment history; or

(5) insurance claims.

(x) Exclusion of Certain Communications for Employee Investigations

(1) A communication is described in this subsection if--

(A) but for subsection (d)(2)(D), the communication would be a consumer report;

(B) the communication is made to an employer in connection with an investigation of–

(i) suspected misconduct relating to employment; or

(ii) compliance with Federal, State, or local laws and regulations, the rules of a self-regulatory organization, or any preexisting written policies of the employer;

(C) the communication is not made for the purpose of investigating a consumer's credit worthiness, credit standing, or credit capacity; and

(D) the communication is not provided to any person except--

(i) to the employer or an agent of the employer;

(ii) to any Federal or State officer, agency, or department, or any officer, agency, or department of a unit of general local government;

(iii) to any self-regulatory organization with regulatory authority over the activities of the employer or employee;

(iv) as otherwise required by law; or

(v) pursuant to section 608.

(2) *Subsequent disclosure.* After taking any adverse action based in whole or in part on a communication described in paragraph (1), the employer

shall disclose to the consumer a summary containing the nature and substance of the communication upon which the adverse action is based, except that the sources of information acquired solely for use in preparing what would be but for subsection (d)(2)(D) an investigative consumer report need not be disclosed.

(3) For purposes of this subsection, the term "self-regulatory organization" includes any self-regulatory organization (as defined in section 3(a)(26) of the Securities Exchange Act of 1934), any entity established under title I of the Sarbanes-Oxley Act of 2002, any board of trade designated by the Commodity Futures Trading Commission, and any futures association registered with such Commission.

§ 604. Permissible purposes of consumer reports [15 U.S.C. § 1681b]

(a) *In general.* Subject to subsection (c), any consumer reporting agency may furnish a consumer report under the following circumstances and no other:

(1) In response to the order of a court having jurisdiction to issue such an order, or a subpoena issued in connection with proceedings before a Federal grand jury.

(2) In accordance with the written instructions of the consumer to whom it relates.

(3) To a person which it has reason to believe

(A) intends to use the information in connection with a credit transaction involving the consumer on whom the information is to be furnished and involving the extension of credit to, or review or collection of an account of, the consumer; or

(B) intends to use the information for employment purposes; or

(C) intends to use the information in connection with the underwriting of insurance involving the consumer; or

(D) intends to use the information in connection with a determination of the consumer's eligibility for a license or other benefit granted by a governmental instrumentality required by law to consider an applicant's financial responsibility or status; or

(E) intends to use the information, as a potential investor or servicer, or current insurer, in connection with a valuation of, or an assessment of the credit or prepayment risks associated with, an existing credit obligation; or

(F) otherwise has a legitimate business need for the information

(i) in connection with a business transaction that is initiated by the consumer; or

(ii) to review an account to determine whether the consumer continues to meet the terms of the account.

(4) In response to a request by the head of a State or local child support enforcement agency (or a State or local government official authorized by the head of such an agency), if the person making the request certifies to the consumer reporting agency that

(A) the consumer report is needed for the purpose of establishing an individual's capacity to make child support payments or determining the appropriate level of such payments;

(B) the paternity of the consumer for the child to which the obligation relates has been established or acknowledged by the consumer in accordance with State laws under which the obligation arises (if required by those laws);

(C) the person has provided at least 10 days' prior notice to the consumer whose report is requested, by certified or registered mail to the last known address of the consumer, that the report will be requested; and

(D) the consumer report will be kept confidential, will be used solely for a purpose described in subparagraph (A), and will not be used in connection with any other civil, administrative, or criminal proceeding, or for any other purpose.

(5) To an agency administering a State plan under Section 454 of the

Social Security Act (42 U.S.C. § 654) for use to set an initial or modified child support award.

(b) Conditions for Furnishing and Using Consumer Reports for Employment Purposes.

(1) *Certification from user.* A consumer reporting agency may furnish a consumer report for employment purposes only if

(A) the person who obtains such report from the agency certifies to the agency that

(i) the person has complied with paragraph (2) with respect to the consumer report, and the person will comply with paragraph (3) with respect to the consumer report if paragraph (3) becomes applicable; and

(ii) information from the consumer report will not be used in violation of any applicable Federal or State equal employment opportunity law or regulation; and

(B) the consumer reporting agency provides with the report, or has previously provided, a summary of the consumer's rights under this title, as prescribed by the Federal Trade Commission under section 609(c)(3) [§ 1681g].[1]

(2) Disclosure to Consumer.

(A) *In general.* Except as provided in subparagraph (B), a person may not procure a consumer report, or cause a consumer report to be procured, for employment purposes with respect to any consumer, unless--

(i) a clear and conspicuous disclosure has been made in writing to the consumer at any time before the report is procured or caused to be procured, in a document that consists solely of the disclosure, that a consumer report may be obtained for employment purposes; and

(ii) the consumer has authorized in writing (which authorization may be made on the document referred to in clause (i)) the procurement of the report by that person.

(B) *Application by mail, telephone, computer, or other similar means.* If a consumer described in subparagraph (C) applies for employment by mail, telephone, computer, or other similar means, at any time before a consumer report is procured or caused to be procured in connection with that application--

(i) the person who procures the consumer report on the consumer for employment purposes shall provide to the consumer, by oral, written, or electronic means, notice that a consumer report may be obtained for employment purposes, and a summary of the consumer's rights under section 615(a)(3); and

(ii) the consumer shall have consented, orally, in writing, or electronically to the procurement of the report by that person.

(C) *Scope.* Subparagraph (B) shall apply to a person procuring a consumer report on a consumer in connection with the consumer's application for employment only if--

(i) the consumer is applying for a position over which the Secretary of Transportation has the power to establish qualifications and maximum hours of service pursuant to the provisions of section 31502 of title 49, or a position subject to safety regulation by a State transportation agency; and

(ii) as of the time at which the person procures the report or causes the report to be procured the only interaction between the consumer and the person in connection with that employment application has been by mail, telephone, computer, or other similar means.

(3) Conditions on use for adverse actions.

(A) *In general.* Except as provided in subparagraph (B), in using a consumer report for employment purposes, before taking any adverse action based in whole or in part on the report, the person intending to take such adverse action shall provide to the consumer to whom the report relates--

(i) a copy of the report; and

(ii) a description in writing of the rights of the consumer under this title, as prescribed by the Federal Trade Commission under section 609(c)(3).1

1The reference in Section 604(b)(1)(B) should be to Section 609(c)**(1)**, not (c)(3) that no longer exists as the result of Congress' re-organization of Section 609(c) in 2003 (FACT Act).)

(B) Application by mail, telephone, computer, or other similar means.

(i) If a consumer described in subparagraph (C) applies for employment by mail, telephone, computer, or other similar means, and if a person who has procured a consumer report on the consumer for employment purposes takes adverse action on the employment application based in whole or in part on the report, then the person must provide to the consumer to whom the report relates, in lieu of the notices required under subparagraph (A) of this section and under section 615(a), within 3 business days of taking such action, an oral, written or electronic notification--

(I) that adverse action has been taken based in whole or in part on a consumer report received from a consumer reporting agency;

(II) of the name, address and telephone number of the consumer reporting agency that furnished the consumer report (including a toll-free telephone number established by the agency if the agency compiles and maintains files on consumers on a nationwide basis);

(III) that the consumer reporting agency did not make the decision to take the adverse action and is unable to provide to the consumer the specific reasons why the adverse action was taken; and

(IV) that the consumer may, upon providing proper identification, request a free copy of a report and may dispute with the consumer reporting agency the accuracy or completeness of any information in a report.

(ii) If, under clause (B)(i)(IV), the consumer requests a copy of a consumer report from the person who procured the report, then, within 3 business days of receiving the consumer's request, together with proper identification, the person must send or provide to the consumer a copy of a report and a copy of the consumer's rights as prescribed by the Federal Trade Commission under section 609(c)(3).

(C) *Scope.* Subparagraph (B) shall apply to a person procuring a consumer report on a consumer in connection with the consumer's application for employment only if--

(i) the consumer is applying for a position over which the Secretary of Transportation has the power to establish qualifications and maximum hours of service pursuant to the provisions of section 31502 of title 49, or a position subject to safety regulation by a State transportation agency; and

(ii) as of the time at which the person procures the report or causes the report to be procured the only interaction between the consumer and the person in connection with that employment application has been by mail, telephone, computer, or other similar means.

(4) Exception for national security investigations.

(A) *In general.* In the case of an agency or department of the United States Government which seeks to obtain and use a consumer report for employment purposes, paragraph (3) shall not apply to any adverse action by such agency or department which is based in part on such consumer report, if the head of such agency or department makes a written finding that–

(i) the consumer report is relevant to a national security investigation of such agency or department;

(ii) the investigation is within the jurisdiction of such agency or department;

(iii) there is reason to believe that compliance with paragraph (3) will--

(I) endanger the life or physical safety of any person;

(II) result in flight from prosecution;

(III) result in the destruction of, or tampering with, evidence relevant to the investigation;

(IV) result in the intimidation of a potential witness relevant to the investigation;

(V) result in the compromise of classified information; or

(VI) otherwise seriously jeopardize or unduly delay the investigation or another official proceeding.

(B) *Notification of consumer upon conclusion of investigation.* Upon the conclusion of a national security investigation described in subparagraph (A), or upon the determination that the exception under subparagraph (A) is no longer required for the reasons set forth in such subparagraph, the official exercising the authority in such subparagraph shall provide to the consumer who is the subject of the consumer report with regard to which such finding was made--

(i) a copy of such consumer report with any classified information redacted as necessary;

(ii) notice of any adverse action which is based, in part, on the consumer report; and

(iii) the identification with reasonable specificity of the nature of the investigation for which the consumer report was sought.

(C) *Delegation by head of agency or department.* For purposes of subparagraphs (A) and (B), the head of any agency or department of the United States Government may delegate his or her authorities under this paragraph to an official of such agency or department who has personnel security responsibilities and is a member of the Senior Executive Service or equivalent civilian or military rank.

(D) *Report to the Congress.* Not later than January 31 of each year, the head of each agency and department of the United States Government that exercised authority under this paragraph during the preceding year shall submit a report to the Congress on the number of times the department or agency exercised such authority during the year.

(E) *Definitions.* For purposes of this paragraph, the following definitions shall apply:

(i) The term "classified information" means information that is protected from unauthorized disclosure under Executive Order No. 12958 or successor orders.

(ii) The term "national security investigation" means any official inquiry by an agency or department of the United States Government to determine the eligibility of a consumer to receive access or continued access to classified information or to determine whether classified information has been lost or compromised.

(c) Furnishing reports in connection with credit or insurance transactions that are not initiated by the consumer.

(1) *In general.* A consumer reporting agency may furnish a consumer report relating to any consumer pursuant to subparagraph (A) or (C) of subsection (a)(3) in connection with any credit or insurance transaction that is not initiated by the consumer only if

(A) the consumer authorizes the agency to provide such report to such person; or

(B)(i) the transaction consists of a firm offer of credit or insurance;

(ii) the consumer reporting agency has complied with subsection (e); and

(iii) there is not in effect an election by the consumer, made in accordance with subsection (e), to have the consumer's name and address excluded from lists of names provided by the agency pursuant to this paragraph.

(2) *Limits on information received under paragraph (1)(B).* A person may receive pursuant to paragraph (1)(B) only

(A) the name and address of a consumer;

(B) an identifier that is not unique to the consumer and that is used by the person solely for the purpose of verifying the identity of the consumer; and

(C) other information pertaining to a consumer that does not identify the relationship or experience of the consumer with respect to a particular creditor or other entity.

(3) *Information regarding inquiries.* Except as provided in section 609(a) (5)

[§1681g], a consumer reporting agency shall not furnish to any person a record of inquiries in connection with a credit or insurance transaction that is not initiated by a consumer.

(d) Reserved.

(e) Election of consumer to be excluded from lists.

(1) *In general.* A consumer may elect to have the consumer's name and address excluded from any list provided by a consumer reporting agency under subsection (c)(1)(B) in connection with a credit or insurance transaction that is not initiated by the consumer, by notifying the agency in accordance with paragraph (2) that the consumer does not consent to any use of a consumer report relating to the consumer in connection with any credit or insurance transaction that is not initiated by the consumer.

(2) *Manner of notification.* A consumer shall notify a consumer reporting agency under paragraph (1)

(A) through the notification system maintained by the agency under paragraph (5); or

(B) by submitting to the agency a signed notice of election form issued by the agency for purposes of this subparagraph.

(3) *Response of agency after notification through system.* Upon receipt of notification of the election of a consumer under paragraph (1) through the notification system maintained by the agency under paragraph (5), a consumer reporting agency shall

(A) inform the consumer that the election is effective only for the 5-year period following the election if the consumer does not submit to the agency a signed notice of election form issued by the agency for purposes of paragraph (2)(B); and

(B) provide to the consumer a notice of election form, if requested by the consumer, not later than 5 business days after receipt of the notification of the election through the system established under paragraph (5), in the case of a request made at the time the consumer provides notification through the system.

(4) *Effectiveness of election.* An election of a consumer under paragraph (1)

(A) shall be effective with respect to a consumer reporting agency beginning 5 business days after the date on which the consumer notifies the agency in accordance with paragraph (2);

(B) shall be effective with respect to a consumer reporting agency

(i) subject to subparagraph (C), during the 5-year period beginning 5 business days after the date on which the consumer notifies the agency of the election, in the case of an election for which a consumer notifies the agency only in accordance with paragraph (2)(A); or

(ii) until the consumer notifies the agency under subparagraph (C), in the case of an election for which a consumer notifies the agency in accordance with paragraph (2)(B);

(C) shall not be effective after the date on which the consumer notifies the agency, through the notification system established by the agency under paragraph (5), that the election is no longer effective; and

(D) shall be effective with respect to each affiliate of the agency.

(5) Notification System

(A) *In general.* Each consumer reporting agency that, under subsection (c)(1)(B), furnishes a consumer report in connection with a credit or insurance transaction that is not initiated by a consumer, shall

(i) establish and maintain a notification system, including a toll-free telephone number, which permits any consumer whose consumer report is maintained by the agency to notify the agency, with appropriate identification, of the consumer's election to have the consumer's name and address excluded from any such list of names and addresses provided by the agency for such a transaction; and

(ii) publish by not later than 365 days after the date of enactment of the Consumer Credit Reporting Reform Act of 1996, and not less than annually thereafter, in a publication of general circulation in the area served by the agency

(I) a notification that information in consumer files maintained by the agency may be used in connection with such transactions; and

(II) the address and toll-free telephone number for consumers to use to notify the agency of the consumer's election under clause (I).

(B) *Establishment and maintenance as compliance.* Establishment and maintenance of a notification system (including a toll-free telephone number) and publication by a consumer reporting agency on the agency's own behalf and on behalf of any of its affiliates in accordance with this paragraph is deemed to be compliance with this paragraph by each of those affiliates.

(6) *Notification system by agencies that operate nationwide.* Each consumer reporting agency that compiles and maintains files on consumers on a nationwide basis shall establish and maintain a notification system for purposes of paragraph (5) jointly with other such consumer reporting agencies.

(f) *Certain use or obtaining of information prohibited.* A person shall not use or obtain a consumer report for any purpose unless

(1) the consumer report is obtained for a purpose for which the consumer report is authorized to be furnished under this section; and

(2) the purpose is certified in accordance with section 607 [§ 1681e] by a prospective user of the report through a general or specific certification.

(g) Protection of Medical Information

(1) *Limitation on consumer reporting agencies.* A consumer reporting agency shall not furnish for employment purposes, or in connection

with a credit or insurance transaction, a consumer report that contains medical information (other than medical contact information treated in the manner required under section 605(a)(6)) about a consumer, unless--

(A) if furnished in connection with an insurance transaction, the consumer affirmatively consents to the furnishing of the report;

(B) if furnished for employment purposes or in connection with a credit transaction--

(i) the information to be furnished is relevant to process or effect the employment or credit transaction; and

(ii) the consumer provides specific written consent for the furnishing of the report that describes in clear and conspicuous language the use for which the information will be furnished; or

(C) the information to be furnished pertains solely to transactions, accounts, or balances relating to debts arising from the receipt of medical services, products, or devises, where such information, other than account status or amounts, is restricted or reported using codes that do not identify, or do not provide information sufficient to infer, the specific provider or the nature of such services, products, or devices, as provided in section 605(a)(6).

(2) *Limitation on creditors.* Except as permitted pursuant to paragraph (3)(C) or regulations prescribed under paragraph (5)(A), a creditor shall not obtain or use medical information (other than medical contact information treated in the manner required under section 605(a)(6)) pertaining to a consumer in connection with any determination of the consumer's eligibility, or continued eligibility, for credit.

(3) *Actions authorized by federal law, insurance activities and regulatory determinations.*

Section 603(d)(3) shall not be construed so as to treat information or any communication of information as a consumer report if the information or communication is disclosed--

(A) in connection with the business of insurance or annuities, including the activities described in section 18B of the model Privacy of Consumer Financial and Health Information Regulation issued by the National Association of Insurance Commissioners (as in effect on January 1, 2003);

(B) for any purpose permitted without authorization under the Standards for Individually Identifiable Health Information promulgated by the Department of Health and Human Services pursuant to the Health Insurance Portability and Accountability Act of 1996, or referred to under section 1179 of such Act, or described in section 502(e) of Public Law 106-102; or

(C) as otherwise determined to be necessary and appropriate, by regulation or order and subject to paragraph (6), by the Commission, any Federal banking agency or the National Credit Union Administration (with respect to any financial institution subject to the jurisdiction of such agency or Administration under paragraph (1), (2), or (3) of section 621(b), or the applicable State insurance authority (with respect to any person engaged in providing insurance or annuities).[2]

The reporting periods have been lengthened for certain adverse information pertaining to U.S. Government insured or guaranteed student loans, or pertaining to national direct student loans. See sections 430A(f) and 463(c)(3) of the Higher Education Act of 1965, 20 U.S.C. 1080a(f) and 20 U.S.C. 1087cc(c)(3), respectively.

(4) *Limitation on redisclosure of medical information.* Any person that receives medical information pursuant to paragraph (1) or (3) shall not disclose such information to any other person, except as necessary to carry out the purpose for which the information was initially disclosed, or as otherwise permitted by statute, regulation, or order.

(5) Regulations and Effective Date for Paragraph (2)

(A) *Regulations required.* Each Federal banking agency and the National Credit Union Administration shall, subject to paragraph (6) and after notice and opportunity for comment, prescribe regulations that permit transactions under paragraph (2) that are determined to be necessary and appropriate to protect legitimate operational, transactional, risk, consumer, and other needs (and which shall include permitting actions necessary for administrative verification purposes), consistent with the intent of paragraph (2) to restrict the use of medical information for inappropriate purposes.

(B) *Final regulations required.* The Federal banking agencies and the National Credit Union Administration shall issue the regulations required under subparagraph (A) in final form before the end of the 6-month period beginning on the date of enactment of the Fair and Accurate Credit Transactions Act of 2003.

(6) *Coordination with other laws.* No provision of this subsection shall be construed as altering, affecting, or superseding the applicability of any other provision of Federal law relating to medical confidentiality.

§ 605. Requirements relating to information contained in consumer reports [15 U.S.C. §1681c]

(a) *Information excluded from consumer reports.* Except as authorized under subsection (b) of this section, no consumer reporting agency may make any consumer report containing any of the following items of information:

(1) Cases under title 11 [United States Code] or under the Bankruptcy Act that, from the date of entry of the order for relief or the date of adjudication, as the case may be, antedate the report by more than 10 years.

(2) Civil suits, civil judgments, and records of arrest that from date of entry, antedate the report by more than seven years or until the governing statute of limitations has expired, whichever is the longer period.

(3) Paid tax liens which, from date of payment, antedate the report by more than seven years.

(4) Accounts placed for collection or charged to profit and loss which antedate the report by more than seven years.

(5) Any other adverse item of information, other than records of

convictions of crimes which antedates the report by more than seven years.2

(6) The name, address, and telephone number of any medical information furnisher that has notified the agency of its status, unless--

(A) such name, address, and telephone number are restricted or reported using codes that do not identify, or provide information sufficient to infer, the specific provider or the nature of such services, products, or devices to a person other than the consumer; or

(B) the report is being provided to an insurance company for a purpose relating to engaging in the business of insurance other than property and casualty insurance.

(b) *Exempted cases.* The provisions of paragraphs (1) through (5) of subsection (a) of this section are not applicable in the case of any consumer credit report to be used in connection with

(1) a credit transaction involving, or which may reasonably be expected to involve, a principal amount of $150,000 or more;

(2) the underwriting of life insurance involving, or which may reasonably be expected to involve, a face amount of $150,000 or more; or

(3) the employment of any individual at an annual salary which equals, or which may reasonably be expected to equal $75,000, or more.

(c) Running of Reporting Period

(1) *In general.* The 7-year period referred to in paragraphs (4) and (6)[3] of subsection (a) shall begin, with respect to any delinquent account that is placed for collection (internally or by referral to a third party, whichever is earlier), charged to profit and loss, or subjected to any similar action, upon the expiration of the 180-day period beginning on the date of the commencement of the delinquency which immediately preceded the collection activity, charge to profit and loss, or similar action.

3This provision, added in September 1996, should read "paragraphs (4) and *(5)* ..." Prior Section 605(a)(6) was amended and re-designated as Section 605(a)(5) in November 1998. The current Section 605(a)(6), added in December 2003 and now containing no reference to any 7-year period, is obviously inapplicable.

(2) *Effective date.* Paragraph (1) shall apply only to items of information added to the file of a consumer on or after the date that is 455 days after the date of enactment of the Consumer Credit Reporting Reform Act of 1996.

(d) Information Required to be Disclosed

(1) *Title 11 information.* Any consumer reporting agency that furnishes a consumer report that contains information regarding any case involving the consumer that arises under title 11, United States Code, shall include in the report an identification of the chapter of such title 11 under which such case arises if provided by the source of the information. If any case arising or filed under title 11, United States Code, is withdrawn by the consumer before a final judgment, the consumer reporting agency shall include in the report that such case or filing was withdrawn upon receipt of documentation certifying such withdrawal.

(2) *Key factor in credit score information.* Any consumer reporting agency that furnishes a consumer report that contains any credit score or any other risk score or predictor on any consumer shall include in the report a clear and conspicuous statement that a key factor (as defined in section 609(f)(2)(B)) that adversely affected such score or predictor was the number of enquiries, if such a predictor was in fact a key factor that adversely affected such score. This paragraph shall not apply to a check services company, acting as such, which issues authorizations for the purpose of approving or processing negotiable instruments, electronic fund transfers, or similar methods of payments, but only to the extent that such company is engaged in such activities.

(e) *Indication of closure of account by consumer.* If a consumer reporting agency is notified pursuant to section 623(a)(4) [§ 1681s-2] that a credit account of a consumer was voluntarily closed by the consumer, the agency shall indicate that fact in any consumer report that includes information related to the account.

(f) *Indication of dispute by consumer.* If a consumer reporting agency is notified pursuant to section 623(a)(3) [§ 1681s-2] that information regarding a consumer who was furnished to the agency is disputed by the consumer, the agency shall indicate that fact in each consumer report that includes the disputed information.

(g) Truncation of Credit Card and Debit Card Numbers

(1) I*n general.* Except as otherwise provided in this subsection, no person that accepts credit cards or debit cards for the transaction of business shall print more than the last 5 digits of the card number or the expiration date upon any receipt provided to the cardholder at the point of the sale or transaction.

(2) *Limitation.* This subsection shall apply only to receipts that are electronically printed, and shall not apply to transactions in which the sole means of recording a credit card or debit card account number is by handwriting or by an imprint or copy of the card.

(3) *Effective date.* This subsection shall become effective--

(A) 3 years after the date of enactment of this subsection, with respect to any cash register or other machine or device that electronically prints receipts for credit card or debit card transactions that is in use before January 1, 2005; and

(B) 1 year after the date of enactment of this subsection, with respect to any cash register or other machine or device that electronically prints receipts for credit card or debit card transactions that is first put into use on or after January 1, 2005.

(h) Notice of Discrepancy in Address

(1) *In general.* If a person has requested a consumer report relating to a consumer from a consumer reporting agency described in section 603(p), the request includes an address for the consumer that substantially differs from the addresses in the file of the consumer, and the agency provides a consumer report in response to the request, the consumer reporting agency shall notify the requester of the existence of the discrepancy.

(2) Regulations

(A) *Regulations required.* The Federal banking agencies, the National Credit Union Administration, and the Commission shall jointly, with respect to the entities that are subject to their respective enforcement authority under section 621, prescribe regulations providing guidance regarding reasonable policies and procedures that a user of a consumer report should employ when such user has received a notice of discrepancy under paragraph (1).

(B) *Policies and procedures to be included.* The regulations prescribed under subparagraph (A) shall describe reasonable policies and procedures for use by a user of a consumer report--

(i) to form a reasonable belief that the user knows the identity of the person to whom the consumer report pertains; and

(ii) if the user establishes a continuing relationship with the consumer, and the user regularly and in the ordinary course of business furnishes information to the consumer reporting agency from which the notice of discrepancy pertaining to the consumer was obtained, to reconcile the address of the consumer with the consumer reporting agency by furnishing such address to such consumer reporting agency as part of information regularly furnished by the user for the period in which the relationship is established.

§ 605A. Identity theft prevention; fraud alerts and active duty alerts [15 U.S.C. §1681c-1]

(a) One-call Fraud Alerts

(1) *Initial alerts.* Upon the direct request of a consumer, or an individual acting on behalf of or as a personal representative of a consumer, who asserts in good faith a suspicion that the consumer has been or is about to become a victim of fraud or related crime, including identity theft, a consumer reporting agency described in section 603(p) that maintains a file on the consumer and has received appropriate proof of the identity of the requester shall--

(A) include a fraud alert in the file of that consumer, and also provide that alert along with any credit score generated in using that file, for a period of not less than 90 days, beginning on the date of such request, unless the consumer or such representative requests that such fraud alert be removed before the end of such period, and the agency has received appropriate proof of the identity of the requester for such purpose; and

(B) refer the information regarding the fraud alert under this paragraph to each of the other consumer reporting agencies described in section 603(p), in accordance with procedures developed under section 621(f).

(2) *Access to free reports.* In any case in which a consumer reporting agency includes a fraud alert in the file of a consumer pursuant to this subsection, the consumer reporting agency shall--

(A) disclose to the consumer that the consumer may request a free copy of the file of the consumer pursuant to section 612(d); and

(B) provide to the consumer all disclosures required to be made under section 609, without charge to the consumer, not later than 3 business days after any request described in subparagraph (A).

(b) Extended Alerts

(1) *In general.* Upon the direct request of a consumer, or an individual acting on behalf of or as a personal representative of a consumer, who submits an identity theft report to a consumer reporting agency described in section 603(p) that maintains a file on the consumer, if the agency has received appropriate proof of the identity of the requester, the agency shall--

(A) include a fraud alert in the file of that consumer, and also provide that alert along with any credit score generated in using that file, during the 7-year period beginning on the date of such request, unless the consumer or such representative requests that such fraud alert be removed before the end of such period and the agency has received appropriate proof of the identity of the requester for such purpose;

(B) during the 5-year period beginning on the date of such request, exclude the consumer from any list of consumers prepared by the consumer reporting agency and provided to any third party to offer credit or insurance to the consumer as part of a transaction that was not initiated by the consumer, unless the consumer or such representative requests that such exclusion be rescinded before the end of such period; and

(C) refer the information regarding the extended fraud alert under this paragraph to each of the other consumer reporting agencies described in section 603(p), in accordance with procedures developed under section 621(f).

(2) *Access to free reports.* In any case in which a consumer reporting agency includes a fraud alert in the file of a consumer pursuant to this subsection, the consumer reporting agency shall--

(A) disclose to the consumer that the consumer may request 2 free copies of the file of the consumer pursuant to section 612(d) during the 12-month period beginning on the date on which the fraud alert was included in the file; and

(B) provide to the consumer all disclosures required to be made under section 609, without charge to the consumer, not later than 3 business days after any request described in subparagraph (A).

(c) *Active duty alerts.* Upon the direct request of an active duty military consumer, or an individual acting on behalf of or as a personal representative of an active duty military consumer, a consumer reporting agency described in section 603(p) that maintains a file on the active duty military consumer and has received appropriate proof of the identity of the requester shall--

(1) include an active duty alert in the file of that active duty military consumer, and also provide that alert along with any credit score generated in using that file, during a period of not less than 12 months, or such longer period as the Commission shall determine, by regulation, beginning on the date of the request, unless the active duty military consumer or such representative requests that such fraud alert be removed before the end of such period, and the agency has received appropriate proof of the identity of the requester for such purpose;

(2) during the 2-year period beginning on the date of such request,

exclude the active duty military consumer from any list of consumers prepared by the consumer reporting agency and provided to any third party to offer credit or insurance to the consumer as part of a transaction that was not initiated by the consumer, unless the consumer requests that such exclusion be rescinded before the end of such period; and

(3) refer the information regarding the active duty alert to each of the other consumer reporting agencies described in section 603(p), in accordance with procedures developed under section 621(f).

(d) *Procedures.* Each consumer reporting agency described in section 603(p) shall establish policies and procedures to comply with this section, including procedures that inform consumers of the availability of initial, extended, and active duty alerts and procedures that allow consumers and active duty military consumers to request initial, extended, or active duty alerts (as applicable) in a simple and easy manner, including by telephone.

(e) *Referrals of alerts.* Each consumer reporting agency described in section 603(p) that receives a referral of a fraud alert or active duty alert from another consumer reporting agency pursuant to this section shall, as though the agency received the request from the consumer directly, follow the procedures required under--

(1) paragraphs (1)(A) and (2) of subsection (a), in the case of a referral under subsection (a)(1)(B);

(2) paragraphs (1)(A), (1)(B), and (2) of subsection (b), in the case of a referral under subsection (b)(1)(C); and

(3) paragraphs (1) and (2) of subsection (c), in the case of a referral under subsection (c)(3).

(f) *Duty of reseller to reconvey alert.* A reseller shall include in its report any fraud alert or active duty alert placed in the file of a consumer pursuant to this section by another consumer reporting agency.

(g) *Duty of other consumer reporting agencies to provide contact information.* If a consumer contacts any consumer reporting agency that is not described in section 603(p) to communicate a suspicion that the consumer has been or is about to become a victim of fraud or related crime, including identity theft, the agency shall provide information to the consumer on how to contact the Commission and the consumer reporting agencies described in section 603(p) to obtain more detailed information and request alerts under this section.

(h) Limitations on Use of Information for Credit Extensions

(1) Requirements for initial and active duty alerts-

(A) *Notification.* Each initial fraud alert and active duty alert under this section shall include information that notifies all prospective users of a consumer report on the consumer to which the alert relates that the consumer does not authorize the establishment of any new credit plan or extension of credit, other than under an open-end credit plan (as defined in section 103(i)), in the name of the consumer, or issuance of an additional card on an existing credit account requested by a consumer, or any increase in credit limit on an existing credit account requested by a consumer, except in accordance with subparagraph (B).

(B) Limitation on Users

(i) *In general.* No prospective user of a consumer report that includes an initial fraud alert or an active duty alert in accordance with this section may establish a new credit plan or extension of credit, other than under an open-end credit plan (as defined in section 103(i)), in the name of the consumer, or issue an additional card on an existing credit account requested by a consumer, or grant any increase in credit limit on an existing credit account requested by a consumer, unless the user utilizes reasonable policies and procedures to form a reasonable belief that the user knows the identity of the person making the request.

(ii) *Verification.* If a consumer requesting the alert has specified a telephone number to be used for identity verification purposes, before authorizing any new credit plan or extension described in clause (i) in the name of such consumer, a user of such consumer report shall contact the consumer using that telephone number or take reasonable steps to verify the consumer's identity and confirm that the application for a new credit plan is not the result of identity theft.

(2) Requirements for Extended Alerts

(A) *Notification.* Each extended alert under this section shall include information that provides all prospective users of a consumer report relating to a consumer with–

(i) notification that the consumer does not authorize the establishment of any new credit plan or extension of credit described in clause (i), other than under an open-end credit plan (as defined in section 103(i)), in the name of the consumer, or issuance of an additional card on an existing credit account requested by a consumer, or any increase in credit limit on an existing credit account requested by a consumer, except in accordance with subparagraph (B); and

(ii) a telephone number or other reasonable contact method designated by the consumer.

(B) *Limitation on users.* No prospective user of a consumer report or of a credit score generated using the information in the file of a consumer that includes an extended fraud alert in accordance with this section may establish a new credit plan or extension of credit, other than under an open-end credit plan (as defined in section 103(i)), in the name of the consumer, or issue an additional card on an existing credit account requested by a consumer, or any increase in credit limit on an existing credit account requested by a consumer, unless the user contacts the consumer in person or using the contact method described in subparagraph (A)(ii) to confirm that the application for a new credit plan or increase in credit limit, or request for an additional card is not the result of identity theft.

§ 605B. Block of information resulting from identity theft [15 U.S.C. §1681c-2]

(a) *Block.* Except as otherwise provided in this section, a consumer reporting agency shall block the reporting of any information in the file of a consumer that the consumer identifies as information that resulted from an alleged identity theft, not later than 4 business days after the date of receipt by such agency of--

(1) appropriate proof of the identity of the consumer;

(2) a copy of an identity theft report;

(3) the identification of such information by the consumer; and

(4) a statement by the consumer that the information is not information relating to any transaction by the consumer.

(b) *Notification.* A consumer reporting agency shall promptly notify the furnisher of information identified by the consumer under subsection (a)--

(1) that the information may be a result of identity theft;

(2) that an identity theft report has been filed;

(3) that a block has been requested under this section; and

(4) of the effective dates of the block.

(c) Authority to Decline or Rescind

(1) *In general.* A consumer reporting agency may decline to block, or may rescind any block, of information relating to a consumer under this section, if the consumer reporting agency reasonably determines that--

(A) the information was blocked in error or a block was requested by the consumer in error;

(B) the information was blocked, or a block was requested by the consumer, on the basis of a material misrepresentation of fact by the consumer relevant to the request to block; or

(C) the consumer obtained possession of goods, services, or money as a result of the blocked transaction or transactions.

(2) *Notification to consumer.* If a block of information is declined or rescinded under this subsection, the affected consumer shall be notified promptly, in the same manner as consumers are notified of the reinsertion of information under section 611(a)(5)(B).

(3) *Significance of block.* For purposes of this subsection, if a consumer reporting agency rescinds a block, the presence of information in the

file of a consumer prior to the blocking of such information is not evidence of whether the consumer knew or should have known that the consumer obtained possession of any goods, services, or money as a result of the block.

(d) Exception for Resellers

(1) *No reseller file.* This section shall not apply to a consumer reporting agency, if the consumer reporting agency--

(A) is a reseller;

(B) is not, at the time of the request of the consumer under subsection (a), otherwise furnishing or reselling a consumer report concerning the information identified by the consumer; and

(C) informs the consumer, by any means, that the consumer may report the identity theft to the Commission to obtain consumer information regarding identity theft.

(2) *Reseller with file.* The sole obligation of the consumer reporting agency under this section, with regard to any request of a consumer under this section, shall be to block the consumer report maintained by the consumer reporting agency from any subsequent use, if--

(A) the consumer, in accordance with the provisions of subsection (a), identifies, to a consumer reporting agency, information in the file of the consumer that resulted from identity theft; and

(B) the consumer reporting agency is a reseller of the identified information.

(3) *Notice.* In carrying out its obligation under paragraph (2), the reseller shall promptly provide a notice to the consumer of the decision to block the file. Such notice shall contain the name, address, and telephone number of each consumer reporting agency from which the consumer information was obtained for resale.

(e) *Exception for verification companies.* The provisions of this section do not apply to a check services company, acting as such, which issues authorizations for the purpose of approving or processing negotiable instruments, electronic fund transfers, or similar methods of payments, except that, beginning 4 business days after receipt of information described in paragraphs (1) through (3) of subsection (a), a check services company shall not report to a national consumer reporting agency described in section 603(p), any information identified in the subject identity theft report as resulting from identity theft.

(f) *Access to blocked information by law enforcement agencies*. No provision of this section shall be construed as requiring a consumer reporting agency to prevent a Federal, State, or local law enforcement agency from accessing blocked information in a consumer file to which the agency could otherwise obtain access under this title.

§ 606. Disclosure of investigative consumer reports [15 U.S.C. § 1681d]

(a) *Disclosure of fact of preparation*. A person may not procure or cause to be prepared an investigative consumer report on any consumer unless

(1) it is clearly and accurately disclosed to the consumer that an investigative consumer report including information as to his character, general reputation, personal characteristics and mode of living, whichever are applicable, may be made, and such disclosure

(A) is made in a writing mailed, or otherwise delivered, to the consumer, not later than three days after the date on which the report was first requested, and

(B) includes a statement informing the consumer of his right to request the additional disclosures provided for under subsection (b) of this section and the written summary of the rights of the consumer prepared pursuant to section 609(c) [§ 1681g]; and

(2) the person certifies or has certified to the consumer reporting agency that

(A) the person has made the disclosures to the consumer required by paragraph (1); and

(B) the person will comply with subsection (b).

(b) *Disclosure on request of nature and scope of investigation.* Any person who procures or causes to be prepared an investigative consumer report on any consumer shall, upon written request made by the consumer within a reasonable period of time after the receipt by him of the disclosure required by subsection (a)(1) of this section, make a complete and accurate disclosure of the nature and scope of the investigation requested. This disclosure shall be made in a writing mailed, or otherwise delivered, to the consumer not later than five days after the date on which the request for such disclosure was received from the consumer or such report was first requested, whichever is the later.

(c) *Limitation on liability upon showing of reasonable procedures for compliance with provisions.* No person may be held liable for any violation of subsection (a) or (b) of this section if he shows by a preponderance of the evidence that at the time of the violation he maintained reasonable procedures to assure compliance with subsection (a) or (b) of this section.

(d) Prohibitions

(1) *Certification.* A consumer reporting agency shall not prepare or furnish investigative consumer report unless the agency has received a certification under subsection (a)(2) from the person who requested the report.

(2) *Inquiries.* A consumer reporting agency shall not make an inquiry for the purpose of preparing an investigative consumer report on a consumer for employment purposes if the making of the inquiry by an employer or prospective employer of the consumer would violate any applicable Federal or State equal employment opportunity law or regulation.

(3) *Certain public record information.* Except as otherwise provided in section 613 [§ 1681k], a consumer reporting agency shall not furnish an investigative consumer report that includes information that is a matter of public record and that relates to an arrest, indictment, conviction, civil judicial action, tax lien, or outstanding judgment, unless the agency has verified the accuracy of the information during the 30-day period ending on the date on which the report is furnished.

(4) *Certain adverse information*. A consumer reporting agency shall not prepare or furnish an investigative consumer report on a consumer that contains information that is adverse to the interest of the consumer and that is obtained through a personal interview with a neighbor, friend, or associate of the consumer or with another person with whom the consumer is acquainted or who has knowledge of such item of information, unless

(A) the agency has followed reasonable procedures to obtain confirmation of the information, from an additional source that has independent and direct knowledge of the information; or

(B) the person interviewed is the best possible source of the information.

§ 607. Compliance procedures [15 U.S.C. § 1681e]

(a) *Identity and purposes of credit users*. Every consumer reporting agency shall maintain reasonable procedures designed to avoid violations of section 605 [§ 1681c] and to limit the furnishing of consumer reports to the purposes listed under section 604 [§ 1681b] of this title. These procedures shall require that prospective users of the information identify themselves, certify the purposes for which the information is sought, and certify that the information will be used for no other purpose. Every consumer reporting agency shall make a reasonable effort to verify the identity of a new prospective user and the uses certified by such prospective user prior to furnishing such user a consumer report.

No consumer reporting agency may furnish a consumer report to any person if it has reasonable grounds for believing that the consumer report will not be used for a purpose listed in section 604 [§ 1681b] of this title.

(b) *Accuracy of report*. Whenever a consumer reporting agency prepares a consumer report it shall follow reasonable procedures to assure maximum possible accuracy of the information concerning the individual about whom the report relates.

(c) *Disclosure of consumer reports by users allowed*. A consumer reporting agency may not prohibit a user of a consumer report furnished by the agency on a consumer from disclosing the contents of the report to the consumer, if adverse action against the consumer has been taken by the user based in whole or in part on the report.

(d) Notice to Users and Furnishers of Information

(1) *Notice requirement.* A consumer reporting agency shall provide to any person

(A) who regularly and in the ordinary course of business furnishes information to the agency with respect to any consumer; or

(B) to whom a consumer report is provided by the agency; a notice of such person's responsibilities under this title.

(2) *Content of notice.* The Federal Trade Commission shall prescribe the content of notices under paragraph (1), and a consumer reporting agency shall be in compliance with this subsection if it provides a notice under paragraph (1) that is substantially similar to the Federal Trade Commission prescription under this paragraph.

(e) Procurement of Consumer Report for Resale

(1) *Disclosure.* A person may not procure a consumer report for purposes of reselling the report (or any information in the report) unless the person discloses to the consumer reporting agency that originally furnishes the report

(A) the identity of the end-user of the report (or information); and

(B) each permissible purpose under section 604 [§ 1681b] for which the report is furnished to the end-user of the report (or information).

(2) *Responsibilities of procurers for resale.* A person who procures a consumer report for purposes of reselling the report (or any information in the report) shall

(A) establish and comply with reasonable procedures designed to ensure that the report (or information) is resold by the person only for a purpose for which the report may be furnished under section 604 [§ 1681b], including by requiring that each person to which the report (or information) is resold and that resells or provides the report (or information) to any other person

(i) identifies each end user of the resold report (or information);

(ii) certifies each purpose for which the report (or information) will be used; and

(iii) certifies that the report (or information) will be used for no other purpose; and

(B) before reselling the report, make reasonable efforts to verify the identifications and certifications made under subparagraph (A).

(3) *Resale of consumer report to a federal agency or department.* Notwithstanding paragraph (1) or (2), a person who procures a consumer report for purposes of reselling the report (or any information in the report) shall not disclose the identity of the end-user of the report under paragraph (1) or (2) if--

(A) the end user is an agency or department of the United States Government which procures the report from the person for purposes of determining the eligibility of the consumer concerned to receive access or continued access to classified information (as defined in section 604(b)(4)(E)(i)); and

(B) the agency or department certifies in writing to the person reselling the report that nondisclosure is necessary to protect classified information or the safety of persons employed by or contracting with, or undergoing investigation for work or contracting with the agency or department.

§ 608. Disclosures to governmental agencies [15 U.S.C. § 1681f]

Notwithstanding the provisions of section 604 [§ 1681b] of this title, a consumer reporting agency may furnish identifying information respecting any consumer, limited to his name, address, former addresses, places of employment, or former places of employment, to a governmental agency.

§ 609. Disclosures to consumers [15 U.S.C. § 1681g]

(a) *Information on file; sources; report recipients.* Every consumer reporting agency shall, upon request, and subject to 610(a)(1) [§ 1681h], clearly and accurately disclose to the consumer:

(1) All information in the consumer's file at the time of the request except that--

(A) if the consumer to whom the file relates requests that the first 5 digits of the social security number (or similar identification number) of the consumer not be included in the disclosure and the consumer reporting agency has received appropriate proof of the identity of the requester, the consumer reporting agency shall so truncate such number in such disclosure; and

(B) nothing in this paragraph shall be construed to require a consumer reporting agency to disclose to a consumer any information concerning credit scores or any other risk scores or predictors relating to the consumer.

(2) The sources of the information; except that the sources of information acquired solely for use in preparing an investigative consumer report and actually use for no other purpose need not be disclosed: Provided, That in the event an action is brought under this title, such sources shall be available to the plaintiff under appropriate discovery procedures in the court in which the action is brought.

(3)(A) Identification of each person (including each end-user identified under section 607(e)(1) [§ 1681e]) that procured a consumer report

(i) for employment purposes, during the 2-year period preceding the date on which the request is made; or

(ii) for any other purpose, during the 1-year period preceding the date on which the request is made.

(B) An identification of a person under subparagraph (A) shall include

(i) the name of the person or, if applicable, the trade name (written in full) under which such person conducts business; and

(ii) upon request of the consumer, the address and telephone number of the person.

(C) Subparagraph (A) does not apply if--

(i) the end user is an agency or department of the United States Government that procures the report from the person for purposes of determining the eligibility of the consumer to whom the report relates to receive access or continued access to classified information (as defined in section 604(b)(4)(E)(i)); and

(ii) the head of the agency or department makes a written finding as prescribed under section 604(b)(4)(A).

(4) The dates, original payees, and amounts of any checks upon which is based any adverse characterization of the consumer, included in the file at the time of the disclosure.

(5) A record of all inquiries received by the agency during the 1-year period preceding the request that identified the consumer in connection with a credit or insurance transaction that was not initiated by the consumer.

(6) If the consumer requests the credit file and not the credit score, a statement that the consumer may request and obtain a credit score.

(b) *Exempt information.* The requirements of subsection (a) of this section respecting the disclosure of sources of information and the recipients of consumer reports do not apply to information received or consumer reports furnished prior to the effective date of this title except to the extent that the matter involved is contained in the files of the consumer reporting agency on that date.

(c) Summary of Rights to Obtain and Dispute Information in Consumer Reports and to Obtain Credit Scores

(1) Commission Summary of Rights Required

(A) *In general.* The Commission shall prepare a model summary of the rights of consumers under this title.

(B) *Content of summary.* The summary of rights prepared under subparagraph (A) shall include a description of–

(i) the right of a consumer to obtain a copy of a consumer report under subsection (a) from each consumer reporting agency;

(ii) the frequency and circumstances under which a consumer is entitled to receive a consumer report without charge under section 612;

(iii) the right of a consumer to dispute information in the file of the consumer under section 611;

(iv) the right of a consumer to obtain a credit score from a consumer reporting agency, and a description of how to obtain a credit score;

(v) the method by which a consumer can contact, and obtain a consumer report from, a consumer reporting agency without charge, as provided in the regulations of the Commission prescribed under section 211(c) of the Fair and Accurate Credit Transactions Act of 2003; and

(vi) the method by which a consumer can contact, and obtain a consumer report from, a consumer reporting agency described in section 603(w), as provided in the regulations of the Commission prescribed under section 612(a)(1)(C).

(C) *Availability of summary of rights.* The Commission shall--

(i) actively publicize the availability of the summary of rights prepared under this paragraph;

(ii) conspicuously post on its Internet website the availability of such summary of rights; and

(iii) promptly make such summary of rights available to consumers, on request.

(2) *Summary of rights required to be included with agency disclosures.* A consumer reporting agency shall provide to a consumer, with each written disclosure by the agency to the consumer under this section--

(A) the summary of rights prepared by the Commission under paragraph (1);

(B) in the case of a consumer reporting agency described in section

603(p), a toll-free telephone number established by the agency, at which personnel are accessible to consumers during normal business hours;

(C) a list of all Federal agencies responsible for enforcing any provision of this title, and the address and any appropriate phone number of each such agency, in a form that will assist the consumer in selecting the appropriate agency;

(D) a statement that the consumer may have additional rights under State law, and that the consumer may wish to contact a State or local consumer protection agency or a State attorney general (or the equivalent thereof) to learn of those rights; and

(E) a statement that a consumer reporting agency is not required to remove accurate derogatory information from the file of a consumer, unless the information is outdated under section 605 or cannot be verified.

(d) Summary of Rights of Identity Theft Victims

(1) *In general.* The Commission, in consultation with the Federal banking agencies and the National Credit Union Administration, shall prepare a model summary of the rights of consumers under this title with respect to the procedures for remedying the effects of fraud or identity theft involving credit, an electronic fund transfer, or an account or transaction at or with a financial institution or other creditor.

(2) *Summary of rights and contact information.* Beginning 60 days after the date on which the model summary of rights is prescribed in final form by the Commission pursuant to paragraph (1), if any consumer contacts a consumer reporting agency and expresses a belief that the consumer is a victim of fraud or identity theft involving credit, an electronic fund transfer, or an account or transaction at or with a financial institution or other creditor, the consumer reporting agency shall, in addition to any other action that the agency may take, provide the consumer with a summary of rights that contains all of the information required by the Commission under paragraph (1), and information on how to contact the Commission to obtain more detailed information.

(e) Information Available to Victims

(1) *In general.* For the purpose of documenting fraudulent transactions resulting from identity theft, not later than 30 days after the date of receipt of a request from a victim in accordance with paragraph (3), and subject to verification of the identity of the victim and the claim of identity theft in accordance with paragraph (2), a business entity that has provided credit to, provided for consideration products, goods, or services to, accepted payment from, or otherwise entered into a commercial transaction for consideration with, a person who has allegedly made unauthorized use of the means of identification of the victim, shall provide a copy of application and business transaction records in the control of the business entity, whether maintained by the business entity or by another person on behalf of the business entity, evidencing any transaction alleged to be a result of identity theft to--

(A) the victim;

(B) any Federal, State, or local government law enforcement agency or officer specified by the victim in such a request; or

(C) any law enforcement agency investigating the identity theft and authorized by the victim to take receipt of records provided under this subsection.

(2) *Verification of identity and claim.* Before a business entity provides any information under paragraph (1), unless the business entity, at its discretion, otherwise has a high degree of confidence that it knows the identity of the victim making a request under paragraph (1), the victim shall provide to the business entity--

(A) as proof of positive identification of the victim, at the election of the business entity--

(i) the presentation of a government-issued identification card;

(ii) personally identifying information of the same type as was provided to the business entity by the unauthorized person; or

(iii) personally identifying information that the business entity typically requests from new applicants or for new transactions, at the time of the victim's request for information, including any documentation described in clauses (i) and (ii); and

(B) as proof of a claim of identity theft, at the election of the business entity--

(i) a copy of a police report evidencing the claim of the victim of identity theft; and

(ii) a properly completed--

(I) copy of a standardized affidavit of identity theft developed and made available by the Commission; or

(II) an affidavit of fact that is acceptable to the business entity for that purpose.

(3) *Procedures.* The request of a victim under paragraph (1) shall--

(A) be in writing;

(B) be mailed to an address specified by the business entity, if any; and

(C) if asked by the business entity, include relevant information about any transaction alleged to be a result of identity theft to facilitate compliance with this section including--

(i) if known by the victim (or if readily obtainable by the victim), the date of the application or transaction; and

(ii) if known by the victim (or if readily obtainable by the victim), any other identifying information such as an account or transaction number.

(4) *No charge to victim.* Information required to be provided under paragraph (1) shall be so provided without charge.

(5) *Authority to decline to provide information.* A business entity may decline to provide information under paragraph (1) if, in the exercise of good faith, the business entity determines that--

(A) this subsection does not require disclosure of the information;

(B) after reviewing the information provided pursuant to paragraph (2), the business entity does not have a high degree of confidence in knowing the true identity of the individual requesting the information;

(C) the request for the information is based on a misrepresentation of fact by the individual requesting the information relevant to the request for information; or

(D) the information requested is Internet navigational data or similar information about a person's visit to a website or online service.

(6) *Limitation on liability.* Except as provided in section 621, sections 616 and 617 do not apply to any violation of this subsection.

(7) *Limitation on civil liability.* No business entity may be held civilly liable under any provision of Federal, State, or other law for disclosure, made in good faith pursuant to this subsection.

(8) *No new recordkeeping obligation.* Nothing in this subsection creates an obligation on the part of a business entity to obtain, retain, or maintain information or records that are not otherwise required to be obtained, retained, or maintained in the ordinary course of its business or under other applicable law.

(9) Rule of Construction

(A) *In general.* No provision of subtitle A of title V of Public Law 106-102, prohibiting the disclosure of financial information by a business entity to third parties shall be used to deny disclosure of information to the victim under this subsection.

(B) *Limitation.* Except as provided in subparagraph (A), nothing in this subsection permits a business entity to disclose information, including information to law enforcement under subparagraphs (B) and (C) of paragraph (1), that the business entity is otherwise prohibited from disclosing under any other applicable provision of Federal or State law.

(10) *Affirmative defense.* In any civil action brought to enforce this subsection, it is an affirmative defense (which the defendant must

establish by a preponderance of the evidence) for a business entity to file an affidavit or answer stating that--

(A) the business entity has made a reasonably diligent search of its available business records; and

(B) the records requested under this subsection do not exist or are not reasonably available.

(11) *Definition of victim.* For purposes of this subsection, the term "victim" means a consumer whose means of identification or financial information has been used or transferred (or has been alleged to have been used or transferred) without the authority of that consumer, with the intent to commit, or to aid or abet, an identity theft or a similar crime.

(12) *Effective date.* This subsection shall become effective 180 days after the date of enactment of this subsection.

(13) *Effectiveness study.* Not later than 18 months after the date of enactment of this subsection, the Comptroller General of the United States shall submit a report to Congress assessing the effectiveness of this provision.

(f) Disclosure of Credit Scores

(1) *In general.* Upon the request of a consumer for a credit score, a consumer reporting agency shall supply to the consumer a statement indicating that the information and credit scoring model may be different than the credit score that may be used by the lender, and a notice which shall include--

(A) the current credit score of the consumer or the most recent credit score of the consumer that was previously calculated by the credit reporting agency for a purpose related to the extension of credit;

(B) the range of possible credit scores under the model used;

(C) all of the key factors that adversely affected the credit score of the consumer in the model used, the total number of which shall not exceed 4, subject to paragraph (9);

(D) the date on which the credit score was created; and

(E) the name of the person or entity that provided the credit score or credit file upon which the credit score was created.

(2) *Definitions.* For purposes of this subsection, the following definitions shall apply:

(A) The term "credit score" --

(i) means a numerical value or a categorization derived from a statistical tool or modeling system used by a person who makes or arranges a loan to predict the likelihood of certain credit behaviors, including default (and the numerical value or the categorization derived from such analysis may also be referred to as a "risk predictor" or "risk score"); and

(ii) does not include--

(I) any mortgage score or rating of an automated underwriting system that considers one or more factors in addition to credit information, including the loan to value ratio, the amount of down payment, or the financial assets of a consumer; or

(II) any other elements of the underwriting process or underwriting decision.

(B) The term "key factors" means all relevant elements or reasons adversely affecting the credit score for the particular individual, listed in the order of their importance based on their effect on the credit score.

(3) *Timeframe and manner of disclosure.* The information required by this subsection shall be provided in the same timeframe and manner as the information described in subsection (a).

(4) *Applicability to certain uses.* This subsection shall not be construed so as to compel a consumer reporting agency to develop or disclose a score if the agency does not--

(A) distribute scores that are used in connection with residential real property loans; or

(B) develop scores that assist credit providers in understanding the general credit behavior of a consumer and predicting the future credit behavior of the consumer.

(5) Applicability to credit scores developed by another person.

(A) *In general.* This subsection shall not be construed to require a consumer reporting agency that distributes credit scores developed by another person or entity to provide a further explanation of them, or to process a dispute arising pursuant to section 611, except that the consumer reporting agency shall provide the consumer with the name and address and website for contacting the person or entity who developed the score or developed the methodology of the score.

(B) *Exception.* This paragraph shall not apply to a consumer reporting agency that develops or modifies scores that are developed by another person or entity.

(6) *Maintenance of credit scores not required.* This subsection shall not be construed to require a consumer reporting agency to maintain credit scores in its files.

(7) *Compliance in certain cases.* In complying with this subsection, a consumer reporting agency shall--

(A) supply the consumer with a credit score that is derived from a credit scoring model that is widely distributed to users by that consumer reporting agency in connection with residential real property loans or with a credit score that assists the consumer in understanding the credit scoring assessment of the credit behavior of the consumer and predictions about the future credit behavior of the consumer; and

(B) a statement indicating that the information and credit scoring model may be different than that used by the lender.

(8) *Fair and reasonable fee.* A consumer reporting agency may charge a fair and reasonable fee, as determined by the Commission, for providing the information required under this subsection.

(9) *Use of enquiries as a key factor.* If a key factor that adversely affects the credit score of a consumer consists of the number of enquiries made with respect to a consumer report, that factor shall be included in the

disclosure pursuant to paragraph (1)(C) without regard to the numerical limitation in such paragraph.

(g) Disclosure of Credit Scores by Certain Mortgage Lenders

(1) *In general.* Any person who makes or arranges loans and who uses a consumer credit score, as defined in subsection (f), in connection with an application initiated or sought by a consumer for a closed end loan or the establishment of an open end loan for a consumer purpose that is secured by 1 to 4 units of residential real property (hereafter in this subsection referred to as the "lender") shall provide the following to the consumer as soon as reasonably practicable:

(A) Information Required under Subsection (f)

(i) *In general.* A copy of the information identified in subsection (f) that was obtained from a consumer reporting agency or was developed and used by the user of the information.

(ii) *Notice under subparagraph (D).* In addition to the information provided to it by a third party that provided the credit score or scores, a lender is only required to provide the notice contained in subparagraph (D).

(B) Disclosures in Case of Automated Underwriting System

(i) *In general.* If a person that is subject to this subsection uses an automated underwriting system to underwrite a loan, that person may satisfy the obligation to provide a credit score by disclosing a credit score and associated key factors supplied by a consumer reporting agency.

(ii) *Numerical credit score.* However, if a numerical credit score is generated by an automated underwriting system used by an enterprise, and that score is disclosed to the person, the score shall be disclosed to the consumer consistent with subparagraph (C).

(iii) *Enterprise defined.* For purposes of this subparagraph, the term "enterprise" has the same meaning as in paragraph (6) of section 1303 of the Federal Housing Enterprises Financial Safety and Soundness Act of 1992.

(C) *Disclosures of credit scores not obtained from a consumer reporting agency.*

A person that is subject to the provisions of this subsection and that uses a credit score, other than a credit score provided by a consumer reporting agency, may satisfy the obligation to provide a credit score by disclosing a credit score and associated key factors supplied by a consumer reporting agency.

(D) *Notice to home loan applicants.* A copy of the following notice, which shall include the name, address, and telephone number of each consumer reporting agency providing a credit score that was used:

"Notice To The Home Loan Applicant

"In connection with your application for a home loan, the lender must disclose to you the score that a consumer reporting agency distributed to users and the lender used in connection with your home loan, and the key factors affecting your credit scores.

"The credit score is a computer generated summary calculated at the time of the request and based on information that a consumer reporting agency or lender has on file. The scores are based on data about your credit history and payment patterns. Credit scores are important because they are used to assist the lender in determining whether you will obtain a loan. They may also be used to determine what interest rate you may be offered on the mortgage. Credit scores can change over time, depending on your conduct, how your credit history and payment patterns change, and how credit scoring technologies change.

"Because the score is based on information in your credit history, it is very important that you review the credit-related information that is being furnished to make sure it is accurate.

"Credit records may vary from one company to another.

"If you have questions about your credit score or the credit information that is furnished to you, contact the consumer reporting agency at the address and telephone number provided with this notice, or contact the lender, if the lender developed or generated the credit score.

"The consumer reporting agency plays no part in the decision to take any action on the loan application and is unable to provide you with specific reasons for the decision on a loan application.

"If you have questions concerning the terms of the loan, contact the lender."

(E) *Actions not required under this subsection.* This subsection shall not require any person to–

(i) explain the information provided pursuant to subsection (f);

(ii) disclose any information other than a credit score or key factors, as defined in subsection (f);

(iii) disclose any credit score or related information obtained by the user after a loan has closed;

(iv) provide more than 1 disclosure per loan transaction; or

(v) provide the disclosure required by this subsection when another person has made the disclosure to the consumer for that loan transaction.

(F) No Obligation for Content

(i) *In general.* The obligation of any person pursuant to this subsection shall be limited solely to providing a copy of the information that was received from the consumer reporting agency.

(ii) *Limit on liability.* No person has liability under this subsection for the content of that information or for the omission of any information within the report provided by the consumer reporting agency.

(G) *Person defined as excluding enterprise.* As used in this subsection, the term

"person" does not include an enterprise (as defined in paragraph (6) of section 1303 of the Federal Housing Enterprises Financial Safety and Soundness Act of 1992).

(2) Prohibition on Disclosure Clauses Null and Void

(A) *In general.* Any provision in a contract that prohibits the disclosure of a credit score by a person who makes or arranges loans or a consumer reporting agency is void.

(B) *No liability for disclosure under this subsection-* A lender shall not have liability under any contractual provision for disclosure of a credit score pursuant to this subsection.

§ 610. Conditions and form of disclosure to consumers [15 U.S.C. § 1681h]

(a) In General

(1) *Proper identification.* A consumer reporting agency shall require, as a condition of making the disclosures required under section 609 [§ 1681g], that the consumer furnish proper identification.

(2) *Disclosure in writing.* Except as provided in subsection (b), the disclosures required to be made under section 609 [§ 1681g] shall be provided under that section in writing.

(b) Other Forms of Disclosure

(1) *In general.* If authorized by a consumer, a consumer reporting agency may make the disclosures required under 609 [§ 1681g]

(A) other than in writing; and

(B) in such form as may be

(i) specified by the consumer in accordance with paragraph (2); and

(ii) available from the agency.

(2) *Form.* A consumer may specify pursuant to paragraph (1) that disclosures under section 609 [§ 1681g] shall be made

(A) in person, upon the appearance of the consumer at the place of business of the consumer reporting agency where disclosures are regularly provided, during normal business hours, and on reasonable notice;

(B) by telephone, if the consumer has made a written request for disclosure by telephone;

(C) by electronic means, if available from the agency; or

(D) by any other reasonable means that is available from the agency.

(c) *Trained personnel.* Any consumer reporting agency shall provide trained personnel to explain to the consumer any information furnished to him pursuant to section 609 [§ 1681g] of this title.

(d) *Persons accompanying consumer.* The consumer shall be permitted to be accompanied by one other person of his choosing, who shall furnish reasonable identification. A consumer reporting agency may require the consumer to furnish a written statement granting permission to the consumer reporting agency to discuss the consumer's file in such person's presence.

(e) *Limitation of liability.* Except as provided in sections 616 and 617 [§§ 1681n and 1681o] of this title, no consumer may bring any action or proceeding in the nature of defamation, invasion of privacy, or negligence with respect to the reporting of information against any consumer reporting agency, any user of information, or any person who furnishes information to a consumer reporting agency, based on information disclosed pursuant to section 609, 610, or 615 [§§ 1681g, 1681h, or 1681m] of this title or based on information disclosed by a user of a consumer report to or for a consumer against whom the user has taken adverse action, based in whole or in part on the report, except as to false information furnished with malice or willful intent to injure such consumer.

§ 611. Procedure in case of disputed accuracy [15 U.S.C. § 1681i]

(a) Reinvestigations of Disputed Information

(1) Reinvestigation Required

(A) *In general.* Subject to subsection (f), if the completeness or accuracy of any item of information contained in a consumer's file at a consumer reporting agency is disputed by the consumer and the consumer notifies the agency directly, or indirectly through a reseller, of such dispute, the agency shall, free of charge, conduct a reasonable reinvestigation to determine whether the disputed information is inaccurate and record the current status of the disputed information, or delete the item from the file in accordance with paragraph (5), before the end of the 30-day period beginning on the date on which the agency receives the notice of the dispute from the consumer or reseller.

(B) *Extension of period to reinvestigate.* Except as provided in subparagraph (C), the 30-day period described in subparagraph (A) may be extended for not more than 15 additional days if the consumer reporting agency receives information from the consumer during that 30-day period that is relevant to the reinvestigation.

(C) *Limitations on extension of period to reinvestigate.* Subparagraph (B) shall not apply to any reinvestigation in which, during the 30-day period described in subparagraph (A), the information that is the subject of the reinvestigation is found to be inaccurate or incomplete or the consumer reporting agency determines that the information cannot be verified.

(2) Prompt Notice of Dispute to Furnisher of Information

(A) *In general.* Before the expiration of the 5-business-day period beginning on the date on which a consumer reporting agency receives notice of a dispute from any consumer or a reseller in accordance with paragraph (1), the agency shall provide notification of the dispute to any person who provided any item of information in dispute, at the address and in the manner established with the person. The notice shall include all relevant information regarding the dispute that the agency has received from the consumer or reseller.

(B) *Provision of other information.* The consumer reporting agency shall promptly provide to the person who provided the information in dispute all relevant information regarding the dispute that is received by the agency from the consumer or the reseller after the period referred to in subparagraph (A) and before the end of the period referred to in paragraph (1)(A).

(3) Determination That Dispute Is Frivolous or Irrelevant

(A) *In general.* Notwithstanding paragraph (1), a consumer reporting agency may terminate a reinvestigation of information disputed by a consumer under that paragraph if the agency reasonably determines that the dispute by the consumer is frivolous or irrelevant, including by reason of a failure by a consumer to provide sufficient information to investigate the disputed information.

(B) *Notice of determination.* Upon making any determination in accordance with subparagraph (A) that a dispute is frivolous or irrelevant, a consumer reporting agency shall notify the consumer of such determination not later than 5 business days after making such determination, by mail or, if authorized by the consumer for that purpose, by any other means available to the agency.

(C) *Contents of notice.* A notice under subparagraph (B) shall include

(i) the reasons for the determination under subparagraph (A); and

(ii) identification of any information required to investigate the disputed information, which may consist of a standardized form describing the general nature of such information.

(4) *Consideration of consumer information.* In conducting any reinvestigation under paragraph (1) with respect to disputed information in the file of any consumer, the consumer reporting agency shall review and consider all relevant information submitted by the consumer in the period described in paragraph (1)(A) with respect to such disputed information.

(5) Treatment of Inaccurate or Unverifiable Information

(A) *In general.* If, after any reinvestigation under paragraph (1) of any information disputed by a consumer, an item of the information is found to be inaccurate or incomplete or cannot be verified, the consumer reporting agency shall–

(i) promptly delete that item of information from the file of the consumer, or modify that item of information, as appropriate, based on the results of the reinvestigation; and

(ii) promptly notify the furnisher of that information that the information has been modified or deleted from the file of the consumer.

(B) Requirements Relating to Reinsertion of Previously Deleted Material

(i) *Certification of accuracy of information.* If any information is deleted from a consumer's file pursuant to subparagraph (A), the information may not be reinserted in the file by the consumer reporting agency unless the person who furnishes the information certifies that the information is complete and accurate.

(ii) *Notice to consumer.* If any information that has been deleted from a consumer's file pursuant to subparagraph (A) is reinserted in the file, the consumer reporting agency shall notify the consumer of the reinsertion in writing not later than 5 business days after the reinsertion or, if authorized by the consumer for that purpose, by any other means available to the agency.

(iii) *Additional information.* As part of, or in addition to, the notice under clause (ii), a consumer reporting agency shall provide to a consumer in writing not later than 5 business days after the date of the reinsertion

(I) a statement that the disputed information has been reinserted;

(II) the business name and address of any furnisher of information contacted and the telephone number of such furnisher, if reasonably available, or of any furnisher of information that contacted the consumer reporting agency, in connection with the reinsertion of such information; and

(III) a notice that the consumer has the right to add a statement to the consumer's file disputing the accuracy or completeness of the disputed information.

(C) *Procedures to prevent reappearance.* A consumer reporting agency shall maintain reasonable procedures designed to prevent the reappearance in a consumer's file, and in consumer reports on the consumer, of information that is deleted pursuant to this paragraph (other than information that is reinserted in accordance with subparagraph (B)(i)).

(D) *Automated reinvestigation system.* Any consumer reporting agency that compiles and maintains files on consumers on a nationwide basis shall implement an automated system through which furnishers of information to that consumer reporting agency may report the results of a reinvestigation that finds incomplete or inaccurate information in a consumer's file to other such consumer reporting agencies.

(6) Notice of Results of Reinvestigation

(A) *In general.* A consumer reporting agency shall provide written notice to a consumer of the results of a reinvestigation under this subsection not later than 5 business days after the completion of the reinvestigation, by mail or, if authorized by the consumer for that purpose, by other means available to the agency.

(B) *Contents.* As part of, or in addition to, the notice under subparagraph (A), a consumer reporting agency shall provide to a consumer in writing before the expiration of the 5-day period referred to in subparagraph (A)

(i) a statement that the reinvestigation is completed;

(ii) a consumer report that is based upon the consumer's file as that file is revised as a result of the reinvestigation;

(iii) a notice that, if requested by the consumer, a description of the procedure used to determine the accuracy and completeness of the information shall be provided to the consumer by the agency, including the business name and address of any furnisher of information contacted in connection with such information and the telephone number of such furnisher, if reasonably available;

(iv) a notice that the consumer has the right to add a statement to the consumer's file disputing the accuracy or completeness of the information; and

(v) a notice that the consumer has the right to request under subsection (d) that the consumer reporting agency furnish notifications under that subsection.

(7) *Description of reinvestigation procedure.* A consumer reporting agency shall provide to a consumer a description referred to in paragraph (6)(B)

(iii) by not later than 15 days after receiving a request from the consumer for that description.

(8) *Expedited dispute resolution.* If a dispute regarding an item of information in a consumer's file at a consumer reporting agency is resolved in accordance with paragraph (5)(A) by the deletion of the disputed information by not later than 3 business days after the date on which the agency receives notice of the dispute from the consumer in accordance with paragraph (1)(A), then the agency shall not be required to comply with paragraphs (2), (6), and (7) with respect to that dispute if the agency

(A) provides prompt notice of the deletion to the consumer by telephone;

(B) includes in that notice, or in a written notice that accompanies a confirmation and consumer report provided in accordance with subparagraph (C), a statement of the consumer's right to request under subsection (d) that the agency furnish notifications under that subsection; and

(C) provides written confirmation of the deletion and a copy of a consumer report on the consumer that is based on the consumer's file after the deletion, not later than 5 business days after making the deletion.

(b) *Statement of dispute.* If the reinvestigation does not resolve the dispute, the consumer may file a brief statement setting forth the nature of the dispute. The consumer reporting agency may limit such statements to not more than one hundred words if it provides the consumer with assistance in writing a clear summary of the dispute.

(c) *Notification of consumer dispute in subsequent consumer reports.* Whenever a statement of a dispute is filed, unless there is reasonable grounds to believe that it is frivolous or irrelevant, the consumer reporting agency shall, in any subsequent report containing the information in question, clearly note that it is disputed by the consumer and provide either the consumer's statement or a clear and accurate codification or summary thereof.

(d) *Notification of deletion of disputed information.* Following any deletion of information which is found to be inaccurate or whose accuracy can no longer be verified or any notation as to disputed information, the consumer reporting agency shall, at the request of the consumer, furnish notification that the item has been deleted or the statement, codification or summary pursuant to subsection (b) or (c) of this section to any person specifically designated by the consumer who has within two years prior thereto received a consumer report for employment purposes, or within six months prior thereto received a consumer report for any other purpose, which contained the deleted or disputed information.

(e) Treatment of Complaints and Report to Congress

(1) *In general.* The Commission shall--

(A) compile all complaints that it receives that a file of a consumer that is maintained by a consumer reporting agency described in section 603(p) contains incomplete or inaccurate information, with respect to which, the consumer appears to have disputed the completeness or accuracy with the consumer reporting agency or otherwise utilized the procedures provided by subsection (a); and

(B) transmit each such complaint to each consumer reporting agency involved.

(2) *Exclusion.* Complaints received or obtained by the Commission pursuant to its investigative authority under the Federal Trade Commission Act shall not be subject to paragraph (1).

(3) *Agency responsibilities.* Each consumer reporting agency described in section 603(p) that receives a complaint transmitted by the Commission pursuant to paragraph (1) shall--

(A) review each such complaint to determine whether all legal obligations imposed on the consumer reporting agency under this title (including any obligation imposed by an applicable court or administrative order) have been met with respect to the subject matter of the complaint;

(B) provide reports on a regular basis to the Commission regarding the determinations of and actions taken by the consumer reporting agency, if any, in connection with its review of such complaints; and

(C) maintain, for a reasonable time period, records regarding the disposition of each such complaint that is sufficient to demonstrate compliance with this subsection.

(4) *Rulemaking authority.* The Commission may prescribe regulations, as appropriate to implement this subsection.

(5) *Annual report.* The Commission shall submit to the Committee on Banking, Housing, and Urban Affairs of the Senate and the Committee on Financial Services of the House of Representatives an annual report regarding information gathered by the Commission under this subsection.

(f) Reinvestigation Requirement Applicable to Resellers

(1) *Exemption from general reinvestigation requirement.* Except as provided in paragraph (2), a reseller shall be exempt from the requirements of this section.

(2) *Action required upon receiving notice of a dispute.* If a reseller receives a notice from a consumer of a dispute concerning the completeness or accuracy of any item of information contained in a consumer report on such consumer produced by the reseller, the reseller shall, within 5 business days of receiving the notice, and free of charge–

(A) determine whether the item of information is incomplete or inaccurate as a result of an act or omission of the reseller; and

(B) if (i) the reseller determines that the item of information is incomplete or inaccurate as a result of an act or omission of the reseller, not later than 20 days after receiving the notice, correct the information in the consumer report or delete it; or

(ii) if the reseller determines that the item of information is not incomplete or inaccurate as a result of an act or omission of the reseller, convey the notice of the dispute, together with all relevant information provided by the consumer, to each consumer reporting agency that provided the reseller with the information that is the subject of the dispute, using an address or a notification mechanism specified by the consumer reporting agency for such notices.

(3) *Responsibility of consumer reporting agency to notify consumer through reseller.* Upon the completion of a reinvestigation under this section of a dispute concerning the completeness or accuracy of any information in the file of a consumer by a consumer reporting agency that received notice of the dispute from a reseller under paragraph (2)--

(A) the notice by the consumer reporting agency under paragraph (6), (7), or (8) of subsection (a) shall be provided to the reseller in lieu of the consumer; and

(B) the reseller shall immediately reconvey such notice to the consumer, including any notice of a deletion by telephone in the manner required under paragraph (8)(A).

(4) *Reseller reinvestigations.* No provision of this subsection shall be construed as prohibiting a reseller from conducting a reinvestigation of a consumer dispute directly.

§ 612. Charges for certain disclosures [15 U.S.C. § 1681j] *See also 16 CFR Part 610 69 Fed. Reg. 35467 (06/24/04)*

(a) Free Annual Disclosure

(1) Nationwide Consumer Reporting Agencies

(A) *In general.* All consumer reporting agencies described in subsections (p) and (w) of section 603 shall make all disclosures pursuant to section 609 once during any 12-month period upon request of the consumer and without charge to the consumer.

(B) *Centralized source.* Subparagraph (A) shall apply with respect to a consumer reporting agency described in section 603(p) only if the request from the consumer is made using the centralized source established for such purpose in accordance with section 211(c) of the Fair and Accurate Credit Transactions Act of 2003.

(C) Nationwide Specialty Consumer Reporting Agency

(i) *In general.* The Commission shall prescribe regulations applicable to each consumer reporting agency described in section 603(w) to require the establishment of a streamlined process for consumers to request consumer reports under subparagraph (A), which shall include, at a minimum, the establishment by each such agency of a toll-free telephone number for such requests.

(ii) *Considerations.* In prescribing regulations under clause (i), the Commission shall consider–

(I) the significant demands that may be placed on consumer reporting agencies in providing such consumer reports;

(II) appropriate means to ensure that consumer reporting agencies can satisfactorily meet those demands, including the efficacy of a system of staggering the availability to consumers of such consumer reports; and

(III) the ease by which consumers should be able to contact consumer reporting agencies with respect to access to such consumer reports.

(iii) *Date of issuance.* The Commission shall issue the regulations required by this subparagraph in final form not later than 6 months after the date of enactment of the Fair and Accurate Credit Transactions Act of 2003.

(iv) *Consideration of ability to comply.* The regulations of the Commission under this subparagraph shall establish an effective date by which each nationwide specialty consumer reporting agency (as defined in section 603(w)) shall be required to comply with subsection (a), which effective date--

(I) shall be established after consideration of the ability of each nationwide specialty consumer reporting agency to comply with subsection (a); and

(II) shall be not later than 6 months after the date on which such regulations are issued in final form (or such additional period not to exceed 3 months, as the Commission determines appropriate).

(2) *Timing.* A consumer reporting agency shall provide a consumer

report under paragraph (1) not later than 15 days after the date on which the request is received under paragraph (1).

(3) *Reinvestigations.* Notwithstanding the time periods specified in section 611(a)(1), a reinvestigation under that section by a consumer reporting agency upon a request of a consumer that is made after receiving a consumer report under this subsection shall be completed not later than 45 days after the date on which the request is received.

(4) *Exception for first 12 months of operation.* This subsection shall not apply to a consumer reporting agency that has not been furnishing consumer reports to third parties on a continuing basis during the 12-month period preceding a request under paragraph (1), with respect to consumers residing nationwide.

(b) *Free disclosure after adverse notice to consumer.* Each consumer reporting agency that maintains a file on a consumer shall make all disclosures pursuant to section 609 [§ 1681g] without charge to the consumer if, not later than 60 days after receipt by such consumer of a notification pursuant to section 615 [§ 1681m], or of a notification from a debt collection agency affiliated with that consumer reporting agency stating that the consumer's credit rating may be or has been adversely affected, the consumer makes a request under section 609 [§ 1681g].

(c) *Free disclosure under certain other circumstances.* Upon the request of the consumer, a consumer reporting agency shall make all disclosures pursuant to section 609 [§ 1681g] once during any 12-month period without charge to that consumer if the consumer certifies in writing that the consumer--

(1) is unemployed and intends to apply for employment in the 60-day period beginning on the date on which the certification is made;

(2) is a recipient of public welfare assistance; or

(3) has reason to believe that the file on the consumer at the agency contains inaccurate information due to fraud.

(d) *Free disclosures in connection with fraud alerts.* Upon the request of a consumer, a consumer reporting agency described in section 603(p) shall make all disclosures pursuant to section 609 without charge to the consumer, as provided in subsections

(a)(2) and (b)(2) of section 605A, as applicable.

(e) *Other charges prohibited* A consumer reporting agency shall not impose any charge on a consumer for providing any notification required by this title or making any disclosure required by this title, except as authorized by subsection (f).

(f) Reasonable Charges Allowed for Certain Disclosures

(1) *In general.* In the case of a request from a consumer other than a request that is covered by any of subsections (a) through (d), a consumer reporting agency may impose a reasonable charge on a consumer

(A) for making a disclosure to the consumer pursuant to section 609 [§ 1681g], which charge

(i) shall not exceed $8;[4] and

4 The Federal Trade Commission increased the maximum allowable charge to $9, effective January 1, 2002. 66 Fed. Reg. 63545 (Dec. 7, 2001).

(ii) shall be indicated to the consumer before making the disclosure; and

(B) for furnishing, pursuant to 611(d) [§ 1681i], following a reinvestigation under section 611(a) [§ 1681i], a statement, codification, or summary to a person designated by the consumer under that section after the 30-day period beginning on the date of notification of the consumer under paragraph (6) or (8) of section 611(a) [§ 1681i] with respect to the reinvestigation, which charge

(i) shall not exceed the charge that the agency would impose on each designated recipient for a consumer report; and

(ii) shall be indicated to the consumer before furnishing such information.

(2) *Modification of amount.* The Federal Trade Commission shall increase the amount referred to in paragraph (1)(A)(I) on January 1 of each year, based proportionally on changes in the Consumer Price Index, with fractional changes rounded to the nearest fifty cents.

§ 613. Public record information for employment purposes [15 U.S.C. § 1681k]

(a) *In general.* A consumer reporting agency which furnishes a consumer report for employment purposes and which for that purpose compiles and reports items of information on consumers which are matters of public record and are likely to have an adverse effect upon a consumer's ability to obtain employment shall

(1) at the time such public record information is reported to the user of such consumer report, notify the consumer of the fact that public record information is being reported by the consumer reporting agency, together with the name and address of the person to whom such information is being reported; or

(2) maintain strict procedures designed to insure that whenever public record information which is likely to have an adverse effect on a consumer's ability to obtain employment is reported it is complete and up to date. For purposes of this paragraph, items of public record relating to arrests, indictments, convictions, suits, tax liens, and outstanding judgments shall be considered up to date if the current public record status of the item at the time of the report is reported.

(b) *Exemption for national security investigations.* Subsection (a) does not apply in the case of an agency or department of the United States Government that seeks to obtain and use a consumer report for employment purposes, if the head of the agency or department makes a written finding as prescribed under section 604(b)(4)(A).

§ 614. Restrictions on investigative consumer reports [15 U.S.C. § 1681*l*]

Whenever a consumer reporting agency prepares an investigative consumer report, no adverse information in the consumer report (other than information which is a matter of public record) may be included in a subsequent consumer report unless such adverse information has been verified in the process of making such subsequent consumer report, or the adverse information was received within the three-month period preceding the date the subsequent report is furnished.

§ 615. Requirements on users of consumer reports [15 U.S.C. § 1681m]

(a) *Duties of users taking adverse actions on the basis of information contained in consumer reports.* If any person takes any adverse action with respect to any consumer that is based in whole or in part on any information contained in a consumer report, the person shall

(1) provide oral, written, or electronic notice of the adverse action to the consumer;

(2) provide to the consumer orally, in writing, or electronically

(A) the name, address, and telephone number of the consumer reporting agency (including a toll-free telephone number established by the agency if the agency compiles and maintains files on consumers on a nationwide basis) that furnished the report to the person; and

(B) a statement that the consumer reporting agency did not make the decision to take the adverse action and is unable to provide the consumer the specific reasons why the adverse action was taken; and

(3) provide to the consumer an oral, written, or electronic notice of the consumer's right

(A) to obtain, under section 612 [§ 1681j], a free copy of a consumer report on the consumer from the consumer reporting agency referred to in paragraph (2), which notice shall include an indication of the 60-day period under that section for obtaining such a copy; and

(B) to dispute, under section 611 [§ 1681i], with a consumer reporting agency the accuracy or completeness of any information in a consumer report furnished by the agency.

(b) Adverse Action Based on Information Obtained from Third Parties Other than Consumer Reporting Agencies

(1) *In general.* Whenever credit for personal, family, or household purposes involving a consumer is denied or the charge for such credit is increased either wholly or partly because of information obtained from a person other than a consumer reporting agency bearing upon the consumer's credit worthiness, credit standing, credit capacity, character, general reputation, personal characteristics, or mode of living, the user of such information shall, within a reasonable period of time, upon the consumer's written request for the reasons for such adverse action received within sixty days after learning of such adverse action, disclose the nature of the information to the consumer. The user of such information shall clearly and accurately disclose to the consumer his right to make such written request at the time such adverse action is communicated to the consumer.

(2) Duties of Person Taking Certain Actions Based on Information Provided by Affiliate

(A) *Duties, generally.* If a person takes an action described in subparagraph (B) with respect to a consumer, based in whole or in part on information described in subparagraph (C), the person shall

(i) notify the consumer of the action, including a statement that the consumer may obtain the information in accordance with clause (ii); and

(ii) upon a written request from the consumer received within 60 days after transmittal of the notice required by clause (I), disclose to the consumer the nature of the information upon which the action is based by not later than 30 days after receipt of the request.

(B) *Action described.* An action referred to in subparagraph (A) is an adverse action described in section 603(k)(1)(A) [§ 1681a], taken in connection with a transaction initiated by the consumer, or any adverse action described in clause (i) or (ii) of section 603(k)(1)(B) [§ 1681a].

(C) *Information described.* Information referred to in subparagraph (A)

(i) except as provided in clause (ii), is information that

(I) is furnished to the person taking the action by a person related by common ownership or affiliated by common corporate control to the person taking the action; and

(II) bears on the credit worthiness, credit standing, credit capacity, character, general reputation, personal characteristics, or mode of living of the consumer; and

(ii) does not include

(I) information solely as to transactions or experiences between the consumer and the person furnishing the information; or

(II) information in a consumer report.

(c) *Reasonable procedures to assure compliance.* No person shall be held liable for any violation of this section if he shows by a preponderance of the evidence that at the time of the alleged violation he maintained reasonable procedures to assure compliance with the provisions of this section.

(d) Duties of Users Making Written Credit or Insurance Solicitations on the Basis of Information Contained in Consumer Files

(1) *In general.* Any person who uses a consumer report on any consumer in connection with any credit or insurance transaction that is not initiated by the consumer, that is provided to that person under section 604(c)(1)(B) [§ 1681b], shall provide with each written solicitation made to the consumer regarding the transaction a clear and conspicuous statement that

(A) information contained in the consumer's consumer report was used in connection with the transaction;

(B) the consumer received the offer of credit or insurance because the consumer satisfied the criteria for credit worthiness or insurability under which the consumer was selected for the offer;

(C) if applicable, the credit or insurance may not be extended if, after the consumer responds to the offer, the consumer does not meet the criteria used to select the consumer for the offer or any applicable criteria bearing on credit worthiness or insurability or does not furnish any required collateral;

(D) the consumer has a right to prohibit information contained in the consumer's file with any consumer reporting agency from being used in connection with any credit or insurance transaction that is not initiated by the consumer; and

(E) the consumer may exercise the right referred to in subparagraph (D) by notifying a notification system established under section 604(e) [§ 1681b].

(2) *Disclosure of address and telephone number; format.* A statement under paragraph (1) shall--

(A) include the address and toll-free telephone number of the appropriate notification system established under section 604(e); and

(B) be presented in such format and in such type size and manner as to be simple and easy to understand, as established by the Commission, by rule, in consultation with the Federal banking agencies and the National Credit Union Administration.

(3) *Maintaining criteria on file.* A person who makes an offer of credit or insurance to a consumer under a credit or insurance transaction described in paragraph (1) shall maintain on file the criteria used to select the consumer to receive the offer, all criteria bearing on credit worthiness or insurability, as applicable, that are the basis for determining whether or not to extend credit or insurance pursuant to the offer, and any requirement for the furnishing of collateral as a condition of the extension of credit or insurance, until the expiration of the 3-year period beginning on the date on which the offer is made to the consumer.

(4) *Authority of federal agencies regarding unfair or deceptive acts or practices not affected.* This section is not intended to affect the authority of any Federal or

State agency to enforce a prohibition against unfair or deceptive acts or practices, including the making of false or misleading statements in connection with a credit or insurance transaction that is not initiated by the consumer.

(e) Red Flag Guidelines and Regulations Required

(1) *Guidelines.* The Federal banking agencies, the National Credit Union Administration, and the Commission shall jointly, with respect to the entities that are subject to their respective enforcement authority under section 621–

(A) establish and maintain guidelines for use by each financial institution and each creditor regarding identity theft with respect to account holders at, or customers of, such entities, and update such guidelines as often as necessary;

(B) prescribe regulations requiring each financial institution and each creditor to establish reasonable policies and procedures for implementing the guidelines established pursuant to subparagraph (A), to identify possible risks to account holders or customers or to the safety and soundness of the institution or customers; and

(C) prescribe regulations applicable to card issuers to ensure that, if a card issuer receives notification of a change of address for an existing account, and within a short period of time (during at least the first 30 days after such notification is received) receives a request for an additional or replacement card for the same account, the card issuer may not issue the additional or replacement card, unless the card issuer, in accordance with reasonable policies and procedures--

(i) notifies the cardholder of the request at the former address of the cardholder and provides to the cardholder a means of promptly reporting incorrect address changes;

(ii) notifies the cardholder of the request by such other means of communication as the cardholder and the card issuer previously agreed to; or

(iii) uses other means of assessing the validity of the change of address, in accordance with reasonable policies and procedures established by the card issuer in accordance with the regulations prescribed under subparagraph (B).

(2) Criteria

(A) *In general.* In developing the guidelines required by paragraph (1)(A), the agencies described in paragraph (1) shall identify patterns, practices, and specific forms of activity that indicate the possible existence of identity theft.

(B) *Inactive accounts.* In developing the guidelines required by paragraph (1)(A), the agencies described in paragraph (1) shall consider including reasonable guidelines providing that when a transaction occurs with respect to a credit or deposit account that has been inactive for more than 2 years, the creditor or financial institution shall follow reasonable policies and procedures that provide for notice to be given to a consumer in a manner reasonably designed to reduce the likelihood of identity theft with respect to such account.

(3) *Consistency with verification requirements.* Guidelines established pursuant to paragraph (1) shall not be inconsistent with the policies and procedures required under section 5318(l) of title 31, United States Code.

(f) Prohibition on Sale or Transfer of Debt Caused by Identity Theft

(1) *In general.* No person shall sell, transfer for consideration, or place for collection a debt that such person has been notified under section 605B has resulted from identity theft.

(2) *Applicability.* The prohibitions of this subsection shall apply to all persons collecting a debt described in paragraph (1) after the date of a notification under paragraph (1).

(3) *Rule of construction.* Nothing in this subsection shall be construed to prohibit--

(A) the repurchase of a debt in any case in which the assignee of the debt requires such repurchase because the debt has resulted from identity theft;

(B) the securitization of a debt or the pledging of a portfolio of debt as collateral in connection with a borrowing; or

(C) the transfer of debt as a result of a merger, acquisition, purchase and assumption transaction, or transfer of substantially all of the assets of an entity.

(g) *Debt collector communications concerning identity theft.* If a person acting as a debt collector (as that term is defined in title VIII) on behalf of a third party that is a creditor or other user of a consumer report is notified that any information relating to a debt that the person is attempting to collect may be fraudulent or may be the result of identity theft, that person shall--

(1) notify the third party that the information may be fraudulent or may be the result of identity theft; and

(2) upon request of the consumer to whom the debt purportedly relates, provide to the consumer all information to which the consumer would otherwise be entitled if the consumer were not a victim of identity theft, but wished to dispute the debt under provisions of law applicable to that person.

(h) Duties of Users in Certain Credit Transactions

(1) *In general.* Subject to rules prescribed as provided in paragraph (6), if any person uses a consumer report in connection with an application for, or a grant, extension, or other provision of, credit on material terms that are materially less favorable than the most favorable terms available to a substantial proportion of consumers from or through that person, based in whole or in part on a consumer report, the person shall provide an oral, written, or electronic notice to the consumer in the form and manner required by regulations prescribed in accordance with this subsection.

(2) *Timing.* The notice required under paragraph (1) may be provided at the time of an application for, or a grant, extension, or other provision of, credit or the time of communication of an approval of an application for, or grant, extension, or other provision of, credit, except as provided in the regulations prescribed under paragraph (6).

(3) *Exceptions.* No notice shall be required from a person under this subsection if—

(A) the consumer applied for specific material terms and was granted those terms, unless those terms were initially specified by the person after the transaction was initiated by the consumer and after the person obtained a consumer report; or

(B) the person has provided or will provide a notice to the consumer under subsection (a) in connection with the transaction.

(4) *Other notice not sufficient.* A person that is required to provide a notice under subsection (a) cannot meet that requirement by providing a notice under this subsection.

(5) *Content and delivery of notice.* A notice under this subsection shall, at a minimum—

(A) include a statement informing the consumer that the terms offered to the consumer are set based on information from a consumer report;

(B) identify the consumer reporting agency furnishing the report;

(C) include a statement informing the consumer that the consumer may obtain a copy of a consumer report from that consumer reporting agency without charge; and

(D) include the contact information specified by that consumer reporting agency for obtaining such consumer reports (including a toll-free telephone number established by the agency in the case of a consumer reporting agency described in section 603(p)).

(6) Rulemaking

(A) *Rules required.* The Commission and the Board shall jointly prescribe rules.

(B) *Content.* Rules required by subparagraph (A) shall address, but are not limited to—

(i) the form, content, time, and manner of delivery of any notice under this subsection;

(ii) clarification of the meaning of terms used in this subsection, including what credit terms are material, and when credit terms are materially less favorable;

(iii) exceptions to the notice requirement under this subsection for classes of persons or transactions regarding which the agencies determine that notice would not significantly benefit consumers;

(iv) a model notice that may be used to comply with this subsection; and

(v) the timing of the notice required under paragraph (1), including the circumstances under which the notice must be provided after the terms offered to the consumer were set based on information from a consumer report.

(7) *Compliance.* A person shall not be liable for failure to perform the duties required by this section if, at the time of the failure, the person maintained reasonable policies and procedures to comply with this section.

(8) Enforcement

(A) *No civil actions.* Sections 616 and 617 shall not apply to any failure by any person to comply with this section.

(B) *Administrative enforcement.* This section shall be enforced exclusively under section 621 by the Federal agencies and officials identified in that section.

§ 616. Civil liability for willful noncompliance [15 U.S.C. § 1681n]

(a) *In general.* Any person who willfully fails to comply with any requirement imposed under this title with respect to any consumer is liable to that consumer in an amount equal to the sum of

(1) (A) any actual damages sustained by the consumer as a result of the failure or damages of not less than $100 and not more than $1,000; or

(B) in the case of liability of a natural person for obtaining a consumer report under false pretenses or knowingly without a permissible purpose, actual damages sustained by the consumer as a result of the failure or $1,000, whichever is greater;

(2) such amount of punitive damages as the court may allow; and

(3) in the case of any successful action to enforce any liability under this section, the costs of the action together with reasonable attorney's fees as determined by the court.

(b) *Civil liability for knowing noncompliance.* Any person who obtains a consumer report from a consumer reporting agency under false pretenses or knowingly without a permissible purpose shall be liable to the consumer reporting agency for actual damages sustained by the consumer reporting agency or $1,000, whichever is greater.

(c) *Attorney's fees.* Upon a finding by the court that an unsuccessful pleading, motion, or other paper filed in connection with an action under this section was filed in bad faith or for purposes of harassment, the court shall award to the prevailing party attorney's fees reasonable in relation to the work expended in responding to the pleading, motion, or other paper.

§ 617. Civil liability for negligent noncompliance [15 U.S.C. § 1681o]

(a) *In general.* Any person who is negligent in failing to comply with any requirement imposed under this title with respect to any consumer is liable to that consumer in an amount equal to the sum of

(1) any actual damages sustained by the consumer as a result of the failure; and

(2) in the case of any successful action to enforce any liability under this section, the costs of the action together with reasonable attorney's fees as determined by the court.

(b) *Attorney's fees.* On a finding by the court that an unsuccessful pleading, motion, or other paper filed in connection with an action under this section was filed in bad faith or for purposes of harassment, the court shall award to the prevailing party attorney's fees reasonable in relation to the work expended in responding to the pleading, motion, or other paper.

§ 618. Jurisdiction of courts; limitation of actions [15 U.S.C. § 1681p]

An action to enforce any liability created under this title may be brought in any appropriate United States district court, without regard to the amount in controversy, or in any other court of competent jurisdiction, not later than the earlier of (1) 2 years after the date of discovery by the plaintiff of the violation that is the basis for such liability; or (2) 5 years after the date on which the violation that is the basis for such liability occurs.

§ 619. Obtaining information under false pretenses [15 U.S.C. § 1681q]

Any person who knowingly and willfully obtains information on a consumer from a consumer reporting agency under false pretenses shall be fined under title 18, United States Code, imprisoned for not more than 2 years, or both.

§ 620. Unauthorized disclosures by officers or employees [15 U.S.C. § 1681r]

Any officer or employee of a consumer reporting agency who knowingly and willfully provides information concerning an individual from the agency's files to a person not authorized to receive that information shall be fined under title 18, United States Code, imprisoned for not more than 2 years, or both.

§ 621. Administrative enforcement [15 U.S.C. § 1681s]

(a) (1) *Enforcement by Federal Trade Commission.* Compliance with the requirements imposed under this title shall be enforced under the Federal Trade Commission Act [15 U.S.C. §§ 41 et seq.] by the Federal Trade Commission with respect to consumer reporting agencies and all other persons subject thereto, except to the extent that enforcement of the requirements imposed under this title is specifically committed to some other government agency under subsection (b) hereof. For the purpose of the exercise by the Federal Trade Commission of its functions and powers under the Federal Trade Commission Act, a violation of any requirement or prohibition imposed under this title shall constitute an unfair or deceptive act or practice in commerce in violation of section 5(a) of the Federal Trade Commission Act [15 U.S.C. § 45(a)] and shall be subject to enforcement by the Federal Trade Commission under section 5(b) thereof [15 U.S.C. § 45(b)] with respect to any consumer reporting agency or person subject to enforcement by the Federal Trade Commission pursuant to this subsection, irrespective of whether that person is engaged in commerce or meets any other jurisdictional tests in the Federal Trade Commission Act. The Federal Trade Commission shall have such procedural, investigative, and enforcement powers, including the power to issue procedural rules in enforcing compliance with the requirements imposed under this title and to require the filing of reports, the production of documents, and the appearance of witnesses as though the applicable terms and conditions of the Federal Trade Commission Act were part of this title. Any person violating any of the provisions of this title shall be subject to the penalties and entitled to the privileges and immunities provided in the Federal Trade Commission Act as though the applicable terms and provisions thereof were part of this title.

(2) (A) In the event of a knowing violation, which constitutes a pattern or practice of violations of this title, the Commission may commence a civil action to recover a civil penalty in a district court of the United States against any person that violates this title. In such action, such person shall be liable for a civil penalty of not more than $2,500 per violation.

(B) In determining the amount of a civil penalty under subparagraph (A), the court shall take into account the degree of culpability, any history of prior such conduct, ability to pay, effect on ability to continue to do business, and such other matters as justice may require.

(3) Notwithstanding paragraph (2), a court may not impose any civil penalty on a person for a violation of section 623(a)(1) [§ 1681s-2] unless the person has been enjoined from committing the violation, or ordered not to commit the violation, in an action or proceeding brought by or on behalf of the Federal Trade Commission, and has violated the

injunction or order, and the court may not impose any civil penalty for any violation occurring before the date of the violation of the injunction or order.

(b) *Enforcement by other agencies.* Compliance with the requirements imposed under this title with respect to consumer reporting agencies, persons who use consumer reports from such agencies, persons who furnish information to such agencies, and users of information that are subject to subsection (d) of section 615 [§ 1681m] shall be enforced under

(1) section 8 of the Federal Deposit Insurance Act [12 U.S.C. § 1818], in the case of

(A) national banks, and Federal branches and Federal agencies of foreign banks, by the Office of the Comptroller of the Currency;

(B) member banks of the Federal Reserve System (other than national banks), branches and agencies of foreign banks (other than Federal branches, Federal agencies, and insured State branches of foreign banks), commercial lending companies owned or controlled by foreign banks, and organizations operating under section 25 or 25A of the Federal Reserve Act [12 U.S.C. §§ 601 et seq., §§ 611 et seq], by the Board of Governors of the Federal Reserve System; and

(C) banks insured by the Federal Deposit Insurance Corporation (other than members of the Federal Reserve System) and insured State branches of foreign banks, by the Board of Directors of the Federal Deposit Insurance Corporation;

(2) section 8 of the Federal Deposit Insurance Act [12 U.S.C. § 1818], by the Director of the Office of Thrift Supervision, in the case of a savings association the deposits of which are insured by the Federal Deposit Insurance Corporation;

(3) the Federal Credit Union Act [12 U.S.C. §§ 1751 et seq.], by the Administrator of the National Credit Union Administration [National Credit Union Administration Board] with respect to any Federal credit union;

(4) subtitle IV of title 49 [49 U.S.C. §§ 10101 et seq.], by the Secretary of Transportation, with respect to all carriers subject to the jurisdiction of the Surface Transportation Board;

(5) the Federal Aviation Act of 1958 [49 U.S.C. Appx §§ 1301 et seq.], by the Secretary of Transportation with respect to any air carrier or foreign air carrier subject to that Act [49 U.S.C. Appx §§ 1301 et seq.]; and

(6) the Packers and Stockyards Act, 1921 [7 U.S.C. §§ 181 et seq.] (except as provided in section 406 of that Act [7 U.S.C. §§ 226 and 227]), by the Secretary of Agriculture with respect to any activities subject to that Act.

The terms used in paragraph (1) that are not defined in this title or otherwise defined in section 3(s) of the Federal Deposit Insurance Act (12 U.S.C. §1813(s)) shall have the meaning given to them in section 1(b) of the International Banking Act of 1978 (12 U.S.C. § 3101).

(c) State Action for Violations

(1) *Authority of states.* In addition to such other remedies as are provided under State law, if the chief law enforcement officer of a State, or an official or agency designated by a State, has reason to believe that any person has violated or is violating this title, the State

(A) may bring an action to enjoin such violation in any appropriate United States district court or in any other court of competent jurisdiction;

(B) subject to paragraph (5), may bring an action on behalf of the residents of the State to recover

(i) damages for which the person is liable to such residents under sections 616 and 617 [§§ 1681n and 1681o] as a result of the violation;

(ii) in the case of a violation described in any of paragraphs (1) through (3) of section 623(c), damages for which the person would, but for section 623(c) [§ 1681s-2], be liable to such residents as a result of the violation; or

(iii) damages of not more than $1,000 for each willful or negligent violation; and

(C) in the case of any successful action under subparagraph (A) or (B), shall be awarded the costs of the action and reasonable attorney fees as determined by the court.

(2) *Rights of federal regulators.* The State shall serve prior written notice of any action under paragraph (1) upon the Federal Trade Commission or the appropriate Federal regulator determined under subsection (b) and provide the Commission or appropriate Federal regulator with a copy of its complaint, except in any case in which such prior notice is not feasible, in which case the State shall serve such notice immediately upon instituting such action. The Federal Trade Commission or appropriate Federal regulator shall have the right

(A) to intervene in the action;

(B) upon so intervening, to be heard on all matters arising therein;

(C) to remove the action to the appropriate United States district court; and

(D) to file petitions for appeal.

(3) *Investigatory powers.* For purposes of bringing any action under this subsection, nothing in this subsection shall prevent the chief law enforcement officer, or an official or agency designated by a State, from exercising the powers conferred on the chief law enforcement officer or such official by the laws of such State to conduct investigations or to administer oaths or affirmations or to compel the attendance of witnesses or the production of documentary and other evidence.

(4) *Limitation on state action while federal action pending.* If the Federal Trade Commission or the appropriate Federal regulator has instituted a civil action or an administrative action under section 8 of the Federal Deposit Insurance Act for a violation of this title, no State may, during the pendency of such action, bring an action under this section against any defendant named in the complaint of the Commission or the

appropriate Federal regulator for any violation of this title that is alleged in that complaint.

(5) Limitations on State Actions for Certain Violations

(A) *Violation of injunction required.* A State may not bring an action against a person under paragraph (1)(B) for a violation described in any of paragraphs (1) through (3) of section 623(c), unless

(i) the person has been enjoined from committing the violation, in an action brought by the State under paragraph (1)(A); and

(ii) the person has violated the injunction.

(B) *Limitation on damages recoverable.* In an action against a person under paragraph (1)(B) for a violation described in any of paragraphs (1) through

(3) of section 623(c), a State may not recover any damages incurred before the date of the violation of an injunction on which the action is based.

(d) *Enforcement under other authority.* For the purpose of the exercise by any agency referred to in subsection (b) of this section of its powers under any Act referred to in that subsection, a violation of any requirement imposed under this title shall be deemed to be a violation of a requirement imposed under that Act. In addition to its powers under any provision of law specifically referred to in subsection (b) of this section, each of the agencies referred to in that subsection may exercise, for the purpose of enforcing compliance with any requirement imposed under this title any other authority conferred on it by law.

(e) Regulatory authority

(1) The Federal banking agencies referred to in paragraphs (1) and (2) of subsection (b) shall jointly prescribe such regulations as necessary to carry out the purposes of this Act with respect to any persons identified under paragraphs (1) and (2) of subsection (b), and the Board of Governors of the Federal Reserve System shall have authority to prescribe regulations consistent with such joint regulations with respect to bank

holding companies and affiliates (other than depository institutions and consumer reporting agencies) of such holding companies.

(2) The Board of the National Credit Union Administration shall prescribe such regulations as necessary to carry out the purposes of this Act with respect to any persons identified under paragraph (3) of subsection (b).

(f) Coordination of Consumer Complaint Investigations

(1) *In general.* Each consumer reporting agency described in section 603(p) shall develop and maintain procedures for the referral to each other such agency of any consumer complaint received by the agency alleging identity theft, or requesting a fraud alert under section 605A or a block under section 605B.

(2) *Model form and procedure for reporting identity theft.* The Commission, in consultation with the Federal banking agencies and the National Credit Union Administration, shall develop a model form and model procedures to be used by consumers who are victims of identity theft for contacting and informing creditors and consumer reporting agencies of the fraud.

(3) *Annual summary reports.* Each consumer reporting agency described in section 603(p) shall submit an annual summary report to the Commission on consumer complaints received by the agency on identity theft or fraud alerts.

(g) *FTC regulation of coding of trade names.* If the Commission determines that a person described in paragraph (9) of section 623(a) has not met the requirements of such paragraph, the Commission shall take action to ensure the person's compliance with such paragraph, which may include issuing model guidance or prescribing reasonable policies and procedures, as necessary to ensure that such person complies with such paragraph.

§ 622. Information on overdue child support obligations [15 U.S.C. § 1681s-1]

Notwithstanding any other provision of this title, a consumer reporting agency shall include in any consumer report furnished by the agency in accordance with section 604 [§ 1681b] of this title, any information on the failure of the consumer to pay overdue support which

(1) is provided

(A) to the consumer reporting agency by a State or local child support enforcement agency; or

(B) to the consumer reporting agency and verified by any local, State, or Federal government agency; and

(2) antedates the report by 7 years or less.

§ 623. Responsibilities of furnishers of information to consumer reporting agencies [15 U.S.C. § 1681s-2]

(a) Duty of Furnishers of Information to Provide Accurate Information

(1) Prohibition

(A) *Reporting information with actual knowledge of errors.* A person shall not furnish any information relating to a consumer to any consumer reporting agency if the person knows or has reasonable cause to believe that the information is inaccurate.

(B) *Reporting information after notice and confirmation of errors.* A person shall not furnish information relating to a consumer to any consumer reporting agency if

(i) the person has been notified by the consumer, at the address specified by the person for such notices, that specific information is inaccurate; and

(ii) the information is, in fact, inaccurate.

(C) *No address requirement.* A person who clearly and conspicuously specifies to the consumer an address for notices referred to in subparagraph (B) shall not be subject to subparagraph (A); however, nothing in subparagraph (B) shall require a person to specify such an address.

(D) *Definition.* For purposes of subparagraph (A), the term "reasonable cause to believe that the information is inaccurate" means having specific knowledge, other than solely allegations by the consumer, that would cause a reasonable person to have substantial doubts about the accuracy of the information.

(2) *Duty to correct and update information.* A person who

(A) regularly and in the ordinary course of business furnishes information to one or more consumer reporting agencies about the person's transactions or experiences with any consumer; and

(B) has furnished to a consumer reporting agency information that the person determines is not complete or accurate, shall promptly notify the consumer reporting agency of that determination and provide to the agency any corrections to that information, or any additional information, that is necessary to make the information provided by the person to the agency complete and accurate, and shall not thereafter furnish to the agency any of the information that remains not complete or accurate.

(3) *Duty to provide notice of dispute.* If the completeness or accuracy of any information furnished by any person to any consumer reporting agency is disputed to such person by a consumer, the person may not furnish the information to any consumer reporting agency without notice that such information is disputed by the consumer.

(4) *Duty to provide notice of closed accounts.* A person who regularly and in the ordinary course of business furnishes information to a consumer reporting agency regarding a consumer who has a credit account with that person shall notify the agency of the voluntary closure of the account by the consumer, in information regularly furnished for the period in which the account is closed.

(5) Duty to Provide Notice of Delinquency of Accounts

(A) *In general.* A person who furnishes information to a consumer reporting agency regarding a delinquent account being placed for collection, charged to profit or loss, or subjected to any similar action shall, not later than 90 days after furnishing the information, notify the agency of the date of delinquency on the account, which shall be the month and year of the commencement of the delinquency on the account that immediately preceded the action.

(B) *Rule of construction.* For purposes of this paragraph only, and provided that the consumer does not dispute the information, a person that furnishes information on a delinquent account that is placed for collection, charged for profit or loss, or subjected to any similar action, complies with this paragraph, if--

(i) the person reports the same date of delinquency as that provided by the creditor to which the account was owed at the time at which the commencement of the delinquency occurred, if the creditor previously reported that date of delinquency to a consumer reporting agency;

(ii) the creditor did not previously report the date of delinquency to a consumer reporting agency, and the person establishes and follows reasonable procedures to obtain the date of delinquency from the creditor or another reliable source and reports that date to a consumer reporting agency as the date of delinquency; or

(iii) the creditor did not previously report the date of delinquency to a consumer reporting agency and the date of delinquency cannot be reasonably obtained as provided in clause (ii), the person establishes and follows reasonable procedures to ensure the date reported as the date of delinquency precedes the date on which the account is placed for collection, charged to profit or loss, or subjected to any similar action, and reports such date to the credit reporting agency.

(6) Duties of Furnishers Upon Notice of Identity Theft-Related Information

(A) *Reasonable procedures.* A person that furnishes information to any consumer reporting agency shall have in place reasonable procedures to respond to any notification that it receives from a consumer reporting agency under section 605B relating to information resulting from identity theft, to prevent that person from refurnishing such blocked information.

(B) *Information alleged to result from identity theft.* If a consumer submits an identity theft report to a person who furnishes information to a consumer reporting agency at the address specified by that person for receiving such reports stating that information maintained by such person that purports to relate to the consumer resulted from identity theft, the person may not furnish such information that purports to relate to the consumer to any consumer reporting agency, unless the person subsequently knows or is informed by the consumer that the information is correct.

(7) Negative Information

(A) Notice to Consumer Required

(i) *In general.* If any financial institution that extends credit and regularly and in the ordinary course of business furnishes information to a consumer reporting agency described in section 603(p) furnishes negative information to such an agency regarding credit extended to a customer, the financial institution shall provide a notice of such furnishing of negative information, in writing, to the customer.

(ii) *Notice effective for subsequent submissions.* After providing such notice, the financial institution may submit additional negative information to a consumer reporting agency described in section 603(p) with respect to the same transaction, extension of credit, account, or customer without providing additional notice to the customer.

(B) Time of Notice

(i) *In general.* The notice required under subparagraph (A) shall be provided to the customer prior to, or no later than 30 days after, furnishing the negative information to a consumer reporting agency described in section 603(p).

(ii) *Coordination with new account disclosures.* If the notice is provided to the customer prior to furnishing the negative information to a consumer reporting agency, the notice may not be included in the initial disclosures provided under section 127(a) of the Truth in

Lending Act.

(C) *Coordination with other disclosures-* The notice required under subparagraph (A)--

(i) may be included on or with any notice of default, any billing statement, or any other materials provided to the customer; and

(ii) must be clear and conspicuous.

(D) Model Disclosure

(i) *Duty of board to prepare.* The Board shall prescribe a brief model disclosure a financial institution may use to comply with subparagraph (A), which shall not exceed 30 words.

(ii) *Use of model not required.* No provision of this paragraph shall be construed as requiring a financial institution to use any such model form prescribed by the Board.

(iii) *Compliance using model.* A financial institution shall be deemed to be in compliance with subparagraph (A) if the financial institution uses any such model form prescribed by the Board, or the financial institution uses any such model form and rearranges its format.

(E) *Use of notice without submitting negative information.* No provision of this paragraph shall be construed as requiring a financial institution that has provided a customer with a notice described in subparagraph (A) to furnish negative information about the customer to a consumer reporting agency.

(F) *Safe harbor.* A financial institution shall not be liable for failure to perform the duties required by this paragraph if, at the time of the failure, the financial institution maintained reasonable policies and procedures to comply with this paragraph or the financial institution reasonably believed that the institution is prohibited, by law, from contacting the consumer.

(G) *Definitions.* For purposes of this paragraph, the following definitions shall apply:

(i) The term "negative information" means information concerning a customer's delinquencies, late payments, insolvency, or any form of default.

(ii) The terms "customer" and "financial institution" have the same meanings as in section 509 Public Law 106-102.

(8) Ability of Consumer to Dispute Information Directly with Furnisher

(A) *In general.* The Federal banking agencies, the National Credit Union Administration, and the Commission shall jointly prescribe regulations that shall identify the circumstances under which a furnisher shall be required to reinvestigate a dispute concerning the accuracy of information contained in a consumer report on the consumer, based on a direct request of a consumer.

(B) *Considerations.* In prescribing regulations under subparagraph (A), the agencies shall weigh--

(i) the benefits to consumers with the costs on furnishers and the credit reporting system;

(ii) the impact on the overall accuracy and integrity of consumer reports of any such requirements;

(iii) whether direct contact by the consumer with the furnisher would likely result in the most expeditious resolution of any such dispute; and

(iv) the potential impact on the credit reporting process if credit repair organizations, as defined in section 403(3) [15 U.S.C. §1679a(3)], including entities that would be a credit repair organization, but for section 403(3)(B)(i), are able to circumvent the prohibition in subparagraph (G).

(C) *Applicability.* Subparagraphs (D) through (G) shall apply in any circumstance identified under the regulations promulgated under subparagraph (A).

(D) *Submitting a notice of dispute-* A consumer who seeks to dispute the accuracy of information shall provide a dispute notice directly to such person at the address specified by the person for such notices that--

(i) identifies the specific information that is being disputed;

(ii) explains the basis for the dispute; and

(iii) includes all supporting documentation required by the furnisher to substantiate the basis of the dispute.

(E) *Duty of person after receiving notice of dispute.* After receiving a notice of dispute from a consumer pursuant to subparagraph (D), the person that provided the information in dispute to a consumer reporting agency shall--

(i) conduct an investigation with respect to the disputed information;

(ii) review all relevant information provided by the consumer with the notice;

(iii) complete such person's investigation of the dispute and report the results of the investigation to the consumer before the expiration of the period under section 611(a)(1) within which a consumer reporting agency would be required to complete its action if the consumer had elected to dispute the information under that section; and

(iv) if the investigation finds that the information reported was inaccurate, promptly notify each consumer reporting agency to which the person furnished the inaccurate information of that determination and provide to the agency any correction to that information that is necessary to make the information provided by the person accurate.

(F) Frivolous or Irrelevant Dispute

(i) *In general.* This paragraph shall not apply if the person receiving a notice of a dispute from a consumer reasonably determines that the dispute is frivolous or irrelevant, including--

(I) by reason of the failure of a consumer to provide sufficient information to investigate the disputed information; or

(II) the submission by a consumer of a dispute that is substantially the same as a dispute previously submitted by or for the consumer, either directly to the person or through a consumer reporting agency under subsection (b), with respect to which the person has already performed the person's duties under this paragraph or subsection (b), as applicable.

(ii) *Notice of determination.* Upon making any determination under clause

(i) that a dispute is frivolous or irrelevant, the person shall notify the consumer of such determination not later than 5 business days after making such determination, by mail or, if authorized by the consumer for that purpose, by any other means available to the person.

(iii) *Contents of notice.* A notice under clause (ii) shall include--

(I) the reasons for the determination under clause (i); and

(II) identification of any information required to investigate the disputed information, which may consist of a standardized form describing the general nature of such information.

(G) *Exclusion of credit repair organizations.* This paragraph shall not apply if the notice of the dispute is submitted by, is prepared on behalf of the consumer by, or is submitted on a form supplied to the consumer by, a credit repair organization, as defined in section 403(3), or an entity that would be a credit repair organization, but for section 403(3)(B)(i).

(9) *Duty to provide notice of status as medical information furnisher.* A person whose primary business is providing medical services, products, or devices, or the person's agent or assignee, who furnishes information to a consumer reporting agency on a consumer shall be considered a medical information furnisher for purposes of this title, and shall notify the agency of such status.

(b) Duties of Furnishers of Information upon Notice of Dispute

(1) *In general.* After receiving notice pursuant to section 611(a)(2) [§ 1681i] of a dispute with regard to the completeness or accuracy of any information provided by a person to a consumer reporting agency, the person shall

(A) conduct an investigation with respect to the disputed information;

(B) review all relevant information provided by the consumer reporting agency pursuant to section 611(a)(2) [§ 1681i];

(C) report the results of the investigation to the consumer reporting agency;

(D) if the investigation finds that the information is incomplete or inaccurate, report those results to all other consumer reporting agencies to which the person furnished the information and that compile and maintain files on consumers on a nationwide basis; and

(E) if an item of information disputed by a consumer is found to be inaccurate or incomplete or cannot be verified after any reinvestigation under paragraph (1), for purposes of reporting to a consumer reporting agency only, as appropriate, based on the results of the reinvestigation promptly–

(i) modify that item of information;

(ii) delete that item of information; or

(iii) permanently block the reporting of that item of information.

(2) *Deadline.* A person shall complete all investigations, reviews, and reports required under paragraph (1) regarding information provided by the person to a consumer reporting agency, before the expiration of the period under section 611(a)(1) [§ 1681i] within which the consumer reporting agency is required to complete actions required by that section regarding that information.

(c) *Limitation on liability.* Except as provided in section 621(c)(1)(B), sections 616 and 617 do not apply to any violation of--

(1) subsection (a) of this section, including any regulations issued thereunder;

(2) subsection (e) of this section, except that nothing in this paragraph shall limit, expand, or otherwise affect liability under section 616 or 617, as applicable, for violations of subsection (b) of this section; or

(3) subsection (e) of section 615.

(d) *Limitation on enforcement.* The provisions of law described in paragraphs (1) through (3) of subsection (c) (other than with respect to the exception described in paragraph (2) of subsection (c)) shall be enforced exclusively as provided under section 621 by the Federal agencies and officials and the State officials identified in section 621.

(e) Accuracy Guidelines and Regulations Required

(1) *Guidelines.* The Federal banking agencies, the National Credit Union Administration, and the Commission shall, with respect to the entities that are subject to their respective enforcement authority under section 621, and in coordination as described in paragraph (2)--

(A) establish and maintain guidelines for use by each person that furnishes information to a consumer reporting agency regarding the accuracy and integrity of the information relating to consumers that such entities furnish to consumer reporting agencies, and update such guidelines as often as necessary; and

(B) prescribe regulations requiring each person that furnishes information to a consumer reporting agency to establish reasonable policies and procedures for implementing the guidelines established pursuant to subparagraph (A).

(2) *Coordination.* Each agency required to prescribe regulations under paragraph (1) shall consult and coordinate with each other such agency so that, to the extent possible, the regulations prescribed by each such entity are consistent and comparable with the regulations prescribed by each other such agency.

(3) *Criteria.* In developing the guidelines required by paragraph (1)(A), the agencies described in paragraph (1) shall--

(A) identify patterns, practices, and specific forms of activity that can compromise the accuracy and integrity of information furnished to consumer reporting agencies;

(B) review the methods (including technological means) used to furnish information relating to consumers to consumer reporting agencies;

(C) determine whether persons that furnish information to consumer reporting agencies maintain and enforce policies to assure the accuracy and integrity of information furnished to consumer reporting agencies; and

(D) examine the policies and processes that persons that furnish information to consumer reporting agencies employ to conduct reinvestigations and correct inaccurate information relating to consumers that has been furnished to consumer reporting agencies.

§ 624. Affiliate sharing [15 U.S.C. § 1681s-3]

(a) Special Rule for Solicitation for Purposes of Marketing

(1) *Notice.* Any person that receives from another person related to it by common ownership or affiliated by corporate control a communication of information that would be a consumer report, but for clauses (i), (ii), and (iii) of section 603(d)(2)(A), may not use the information to make a solicitation for marketing purposes to a consumer about its products or services, unless--

(A) it is clearly and conspicuously disclosed to the consumer that the information may be communicated among such persons for purposes of making such solicitations to the consumer; and

(B) the consumer is provided an opportunity and a simple method to prohibit the making of such solicitations to the consumer by such person.

(2) Consumer Choice

(A) *In general.* The notice required under paragraph (1) shall allow the consumer the opportunity to prohibit all solicitations referred to in such paragraph, and may allow the consumer to choose from different options when electing to prohibit the sending of such solicitations, including options regarding the types of entities and information covered, and which methods of delivering solicitations the consumer elects to prohibit.

(B) *Format.* Notwithstanding subparagraph (A), the notice required under paragraph (1) shall be clear, conspicuous, and concise, and any method provided under paragraph (1)(B) shall be simple. The regulations prescribed to implement this section shall provide specific guidance regarding how to comply with such standards.

(3) Duration

(A) *In general.* The election of a consumer pursuant to paragraph (1)(B) to prohibit the making of solicitations shall be effective for at least 5 years, beginning on the date on which the person receives the election of the consumer, unless the consumer requests that such election be revoked.

(B) *Notice upon expiration of effective period.* At such time as the election of a consumer pursuant to paragraph (1)(B) is no longer effective, a person may not use information that the person receives in the manner described in paragraph (1) to make any solicitation for marketing purposes to the consumer, unless the consumer receives a notice and an opportunity, using a simple method, to extend the opt-out for another period of at least 5 years, pursuant to the procedures described in paragraph (1).

(4) *Scope.* This section shall not apply to a person–

(A) using information to make a solicitation for marketing purposes to a consumer with whom the person has a pre-existing business relationship;

(B) using information to facilitate communications to an individual for whose benefit the person provides employee benefit or other services pursuant to a contract with an employer related to and arising out of the current employment relationship or status of the individual as a participant or beneficiary of an employee benefit plan;

(C) using information to perform services on behalf of another person related by common ownership or affiliated by corporate control, except that this subparagraph shall not be construed as permitting a person to send solicitations on behalf of another person, if such other person would not be permitted to send the solicitation on its own behalf as a result of the election of the consumer to prohibit solicitations under paragraph (1)(B);

(D) using information in response to a communication initiated by the consumer;

(E) using information in response to solicitations authorized or requested by the consumer; or

(F) if compliance with this section by that person would prevent compliance by that person with any provision of State insurance laws pertaining to unfair discrimination in any State in which the person is lawfully doing business.

(5) *No retroactivity.* This subsection shall not prohibit the use of information to send a solicitation to a consumer if such information was received prior to the date on which persons are required to comply with regulations implementing this subsection.

(b) *Notice for other purposes permissible.* A notice or other disclosure under this section may be coordinated and consolidated with any other notice required to be issued under any other provision of law by a person that is subject to this section, and a notice or other disclosure that is equivalent to the notice required by subsection (a), and that is provided by a person described in subsection (a) to a consumer together with disclosures required by any other provision of law, shall satisfy the requirements of subsection (a).

(c) *User requirements.* Requirements with respect to the use by a person of information received from another person related to it by common ownership or affiliated by corporate control, such as the requirements of this section, constitute requirements with respect to the exchange of information among persons affiliated by common ownership or common corporate control, within the meaning of section 625(b)(2).

(d) *Definitions.* For purposes of this section, the following definitions shall apply:

(1) The term "pre-existing business relationship" means a relationship between a person, or a person's licensed agent, and a consumer, based on--

(A) a financial contract between a person and a consumer which is in force;

(B) the purchase, rental, or lease by the consumer of that person's goods or services, or a financial transaction (including holding an active account or a policy in force or having another continuing relationship) between the consumer and that person during the 18-month period immediately preceding the date on which the consumer is sent a solicitation covered by this section;

(C) an inquiry or application by the consumer regarding a product or service offered by that person, during the 3-month period immediately preceding the date on which the consumer is sent a solicitation covered by this section; or

(D) any other pre-existing customer relationship defined in the regulations implementing this section.

(2) The term "solicitation" means the marketing of a product or service initiated by a person to a particular consumer that is based on an exchange of information described in subsection (a), and is intended to encourage the consumer to purchase such product or service, but does not include communications that are directed at the general public or determined not to be a solicitation by the regulations prescribed under this section.

§ 625. Relation to State laws [15 U.S.C. § 1681t]

(a) *In general.* Except as provided in subsections (b) and (c), this title does not annul, alter, affect, or exempt any person subject to the provisions of this title from complying with the laws of any State with respect to the collection, distribution, or use of any information on consumers, or for the prevention or mitigation of identity theft, except to the extent that those laws are inconsistent with any provision of this title, and then only to the extent of the inconsistency.

(b) *General exceptions.* No requirement or prohibition may be imposed under the laws of any State

(1) with respect to any subject matter regulated under

(A) subsection (c) or (e) of section 604 [§ 1681b], relating to the prescreening of consumer reports;

(B) section 611 [§ 1681i], relating to the time by which a consumer reporting agency must take any action, including the provision of notification to a consumer or other person, in any procedure related to the disputed accuracy of information in a consumer's file, except that this subparagraph shall not apply to any State law in effect on the date of enactment of the Consumer Credit Reporting Reform Act of 1996;

(C) subsections (a) and (b) of section 615 [§ 1681m], relating to the duties of a person who takes any adverse action with respect to a consumer;

(D) section 615(d) [§ 1681m], relating to the duties of persons who use a consumer report of a consumer in connection with any credit or insurance transaction that is not initiated by the consumer and that consists of a firm offer of credit or insurance;

(E) section 605 [§ 1681c], relating to information contained in consumer reports, except that this subparagraph shall not apply to any State law in effect on the date of enactment of the Consumer Credit Reporting Reform Act of 1996;

(F) section 623 [§ 1681s-2], relating to the responsibilities of persons who furnish information to consumer reporting agencies, except that this paragraph shall not apply

(i) with respect to section 54A(a) of chapter 93 of the Massachusetts Annotated Laws (as in effect on the date of enactment of the Consumer Credit Reporting Reform Act of 1996); or

(ii) with respect to section 1785.25(a) of the California Civil Code (as in effect on the date of enactment of the Consumer Credit Reporting Reform Act of 1996);

(G) section 609(e), relating to information available to victims under section 609(e);

(H) section 624, relating to the exchange and use of information to make a solicitation for marketing purposes; or

(I) section 615(h), relating to the duties of users of consumer reports to provide notice with respect to terms in certain credit transactions;

(2) with respect to the exchange of information among persons affiliated by common ownership or common corporate control, except that this paragraph shall not apply with respect to subsection (a) or (c)(1) of section 2480e of title 9, Vermont Statutes Annotated (as in effect on the date of enactment of the Consumer Credit Reporting Reform Act of 1996);

(3) with respect to the disclosures required to be made under subsection (c), (d), (e), or (g) of section 609, or subsection (f) of section 609 relating to the disclosure of credit scores for credit granting purposes, except that this paragraph--

(A) shall not apply with respect to sections 1785.10, 1785.16, and 1785.20.2 of the California Civil Code (as in effect on the date of enactment of the Fair and Accurate Credit Transactions Act of 2003) and section 1785.15 through section 1785.15.2 of such Code (as in effect on such date);

(B) shall not apply with respect to sections 5-3-106(2) and 212-14.3-104.3 of the Colorado Revised Statutes (as in effect on the date of enactment of the Fair and Accurate Credit Transactions Act of 2003); and

(C) shall not be construed as limiting, annulling, affecting, or superseding any provision of the laws of any State regulating the use in an insurance activity, or regulating disclosures concerning such use, of a credit-based insurance score of a consumer by any person engaged in the business of insurance;

(4) with respect to the frequency of any disclosure under section 612(a), except that this paragraph shall not apply–

(A) with respect to section 12-14.3-105(1)(d) of the Colorado Revised Statutes (as in effect on the date of enactment of the Fair and Accurate Credit Transactions Act of 2003);

(B) with respect to section 10-1-393(29)(C) of the Georgia Code (as in effect on the date of enactment of the Fair and Accurate Credit Transactions Act of 2003);

(C) with respect to section 1316.2 of title 10 of the Maine Revised Statutes (as in effect on the date of enactment of the Fair and Accurate Credit Transactions Act of 2003);

(D) with respect to sections 14-1209(a)(1) and 14-1209(b)(1)(i) of the Commercial Law Article of the Code of Maryland (as in effect on the date of enactment of the Fair and Accurate Credit Transactions Act of 2003);

(E) with respect to section 59(d) and section 59(e) of chapter 93 of the General Laws of Massachusetts (as in effect on the date of enactment of the Fair and Accurate Credit Transactions Act of 2003);

(F) with respect to section 56:11-37.10(a)(1) of the New Jersey Revised Statutes (as in effect on the date of enactment of the Fair and Accurate Credit Transactions Act of 2003); or

(G) with respect to section 2480c(a)(1) of title 9 of the Vermont Statutes Annotated (as in effect on the date of enactment of the Fair and Accurate Credit Transactions Act of 2003); or

(5) with respect to the conduct required by the specific provisions of--

(A) section 605(g);

(B) section 605A;

(C) section 605B;

(D) section 609(a)(1)(A);

(E) section 612(a);

(F) subsections (e), (f), and (g) of section 615;

(G) section 621(f);

(H) section 623(a)(6); or

(I) section 628.

(c) *Definition of firm offer of credit or insurance.* Notwithstanding any definition of the term "firm offer of credit or insurance" (or any equivalent term) under the laws of any State, the definition of that term contained in section 603(*l*) [§ 1681a] shall be construed to apply in the enforcement and interpretation of the laws of any State governing consumer reports.

(d) *Limitations.* Subsections (b) and (c) do not affect any settlement, agreement, or consent judgment between any State Attorney General and any consumer reporting agency in effect on the date of enactment of the Consumer Credit Reporting Reform Act of 1996.

§ 626. Disclosures to FBI for counterintelligence purposes [15 U.S.C. § 1681u]

(a) *Identity of financial institutions.* Notwithstanding section 604 [§ 1681b] or any other provision of this title, a consumer reporting agency shall furnish to the Federal Bureau of Investigation the names and addresses of all financial institutions (as that term is defined in section 1101 of the Right to Financial Privacy Act of 1978 [12 U.S.C. § 3401]) at which a consumer maintains or has maintained an account, to the extent that information is in the files of the agency, when presented with a written request for that information, signed by the Director of the Federal Bureau of Investigation, or the Director's designee in a position not lower than Deputy Assistant Director at Bureau headquarters or a Special Agent in Charge of a Bureau field office designated by the Director, which certifies compliance with this section. The Director or the Director's designee may make such a certification only if the Director or the Director's designee has determined in writing, that such information is sought for the conduct of an authorized investigation to protect against international terrorism or clandestine intelligence activities, provided that such an investigation of a United States person is not conducted solely upon the basis of activities protected by the first amendment to the Constitution of the United States.

(b) *Identifying information.* Notwithstanding the provisions of section 604 [§ 1681b] or any other provision of this title, a consumer reporting agency shall furnish identifying information respecting a consumer, limited to name, address, former addresses, places of employment, or former places of employment, to the Federal Bureau of Investigation when presented with a written request, signed by the Director or the Director's designee, which certifies compliance with this subsection. The Director or the Director's designee in a position not lower than Deputy Assistant Director at Bureau headquarters or a Special Agent in Charge of a Bureau field office designated by the Director may make such a certification only if the Director or the Director's designee has determined in writing that such information is sought for the conduct of an authorized investigation to protect against international terrorism or clandestine intelligence activities, provided that such an investigation of a United States person is not conducted solely upon the basis of activities protected by the first amendment to the Constitution of the United States.

(c) *Court order for disclosure of consumer reports.* Notwithstanding section 604 [§ 1681b] or any other provision of this title, if requested in writing by the Director of the Federal Bureau of Investigation, or a designee of the Director in a position not lower than Deputy Assistant Director at Bureau headquarters or a Special Agent in Charge of a Bureau field office designated by the Director, a court may issue an order ex parte directing a consumer reporting agency to furnish a consumer report to the Federal Bureau of Investigation, upon a showing in camera that the consumer report is sought for the conduct of an authorized investigation to protect against international terrorism or clandestine intelligence activities, provided that such an investigation of a United States person is not conducted solely upon the basis of activities protected by the first amendment to the Constitution of the United States.

The terms of an order issued under this subsection shall not disclose that the order is issued for purposes of a counterintelligence investigation.

(d) *Confidentiality.* No consumer reporting agency or officer, employee, or agent of a consumer reporting agency shall disclose to any person, other than those officers, employees, or agents of a consumer reporting agency necessary to fulfill the requirement to disclose information to the Federal Bureau of Investigation under this section, that the Federal Bureau of Investigation has sought or obtained the identity of financial institutions or a consumer report respecting any consumer under subsection (a), (b), or (c), and no consumer reporting agency or officer, employee, or agent of a consumer reporting agency shall include in any consumer report any information that would indicate that the Federal Bureau of Investigation has sought or obtained such information or a consumer report.

(e) *Payment of fees.* The Federal Bureau of Investigation shall, subject to the availability of appropriations, pay to the consumer reporting agency assembling or providing report or information in accordance with procedures established under this section a fee for reimbursement for such costs as are reasonably necessary and which have been directly incurred in searching, reproducing, or transporting books, papers, records, or other data required or requested to be produced under this section.

(f) *Limit on dissemination.* The Federal Bureau of Investigation may not disseminate information obtained pursuant to this section outside of the Federal Bureau of Investigation, except to other Federal agencies as may be necessary for the approval or conduct of a foreign counterintelligence investigation, or, where the information concerns a person subject to the Uniform Code of Military Justice, to appropriate investigative authorities within the military department concerned as may be necessary for the conduct of a joint foreign counterintelligence investigation.

(g) *Rules of construction.* Nothing in this section shall be construed to prohibit information from being furnished by the Federal Bureau of Investigation pursuant to a subpoena or court order, in connection with a judicial or administrative proceeding to enforce the provisions of this Act. Nothing in this section shall be construed to authorize or permit the withholding of information from the Congress.

(h) *Reports to Congress.* On a semiannual basis, the Attorney General shall fully inform the Permanent Select Committee on Intelligence and the Committee on Banking, Finance and Urban Affairs of the House of Representatives, and the Select Committee on Intelligence and the Committee on Banking, Housing, and Urban Affairs of the Senate concerning all requests made pursuant to subsections (a), (b), and (c).

(i) *Damages.* Any agency or department of the United States obtaining or disclosing any consumer reports, records, or information contained therein in violation of this section is liable to the consumer to whom such consumer reports, records, or information relate in an amount equal to the sum of

(1) $100, without regard to the volume of consumer reports, records, or information involved;

(2) any actual damages sustained by the consumer as a result of the disclosure;

(3) if the violation is found to have been willful or intentional, such punitive damages as a court may allow; and

(4) in the case of any successful action to enforce liability under this subsection, the costs of the action, together with reasonable attorney fees, as determined by the court.

(j) *Disciplinary actions for violations.* If a court determines that any agency or department of the United States has violated any provision of this section and the court finds that the circumstances surrounding the violation raise questions of whether or not an officer or employee of the agency or department acted willfully or intentionally with respect to the violation, the agency or department shall promptly initiate a proceeding to determine whether or not disciplinary action is warranted against the officer or employee who was responsible for the violation.

(k) *Good-faith exception.* Notwithstanding any other provision of this title, any consumer reporting agency or agent or employee thereof making disclosure of consumer reports or identifying information pursuant to this subsection in good-faith reliance upon a certification of the Federal Bureau of Investigation pursuant to provisions of this section shall not be liable to any person for such disclosure under this title, the constitution of any State, or any law or regulation of any State or any political subdivision of any State.

(l) *Limitation of remedies.* Notwithstanding any other provision of this title, the remedies and sanctions set forth in this section shall be the only judicial remedies and sanctions for violation of this section.

(m) *Injunctive relief.* In addition to any other remedy contained in this section, injunctive relief shall be available to require compliance with the procedures of this section. In the event of any successful action under this subsection, costs together with reasonable attorney fees, as determined by the court, may be recovered.

§ 627. Disclosures to governmental agencies for counterterrorism purposes [15 U.S.C. §1681v]

(a) *Disclosure.* Notwithstanding section 604 or any other provision of this title, a consumer reporting agency shall furnish a consumer report of a consumer and all other information in a consumer's file to a government agency authorized to conduct investigations of, or intelligence or counterintelligence activities or analysis related to, international terrorism when presented with a written certification by such government agency that such information is necessary for the agency's conduct or such investigation, activity or analysis.

(b) *Form of certification.* The certification described in subsection (a) shall be signed by a supervisory official designated by the head of a Federal agency or an officer of a Federal agency whose appointment to office is required to be made by the President, by and with the advice and consent of the Senate.

(c) *Confidentiality.* No consumer reporting agency, or officer, employee, or agent of such consumer reporting agency, shall disclose to any person, or specify in any consumer report, that a government agency has sought or obtained access to information under subsection (a).

(d) *Rule of construction.* Nothing in section 626 shall be construed to limit the authority of the Director of the Federal Bureau of Investigation under this section.

(e) *Safe harbor.* Notwithstanding any other provision of this title, any consumer reporting agency or agent or employee thereof making disclosure of consumer reports or other information pursuant to this section in good-faith reliance upon a certification of a governmental agency pursuant to the provisions of this section shall not be liable to any person for such disclosure under this subchapter, the constitution of any State, or any law or regulation of any State or any political subdivision of any State.

§ 628. Disposal of records [15 U.S.C. §1681w]

(a) Regulations

(1) *In general.* Not later than 1 year after the date of enactment of this section, the Federal banking agencies, the National Credit Union Administration, and the Commission with respect to the entities that are subject to their respective enforcement authority under section 621, and the Securities and Exchange Commission, and in coordination as described in paragraph (2), shall issue final regulations requiring any person that maintains or otherwise possesses consumer information, or any compilation of consumer information, derived from consumer reports for a business purpose to properly dispose of any such information or compilation.

(2) *Coordination.* Each agency required to prescribe regulations under paragraph (1) shall–

(A) consult and coordinate with each other such agency so that, to the extent possible, the regulations prescribed by each such agency are consistent and comparable with the regulations by each such other agency; and

(B) ensure that such regulations are consistent with the requirements and regulations issued pursuant to Public Law 106-102 and other provisions of Federal law.

(3) *Exemption authority.* In issuing regulations under this section, the Federal banking agencies, the National Credit Union Administration, the Commission, and the Securities and Exchange Commission may exempt any person or class of persons from application of those regulations, as such agency deems appropriate to carry out the purpose of this section.

(b) *Rule of construction.* Nothing in this section shall be construed--

(1) to require a person to maintain or destroy any record pertaining to a consumer that is not imposed under other law; or

(2) to alter or affect any requirement imposed under any other provision of law to maintain or destroy such a record.

§ 629. Corporate and technological circumvention prohibited [15 U.S.C. §1681x]

The Commission shall prescribe regulations, to become effective not later than 90 days after the date of enactment of this section, to prevent a consumer reporting agency from circumventing or evading treatment as a consumer reporting agency described in section 603(p) for purposes of this title, including--

(1) by means of a corporate reorganization or restructuring, including a merger, acquisition, dissolution, divestiture, or asset sale of a consumer reporting agency; or

(2) by maintaining or merging public record and credit account information in a manner that is substantially equivalent to that described in paragraphs (1) and (2) of section 603(p), in the manner described in section 603(p).

See also 16 CFR Part 611

69 Fed. Reg. 8531 (02/24/04)

69 Fed. Reg. 29061 (05/20/04)

Legislative History

House Reports: No. 91-975 (Comm. on Banking and Currency) and No. 91-1587 (Comm. of Conference)

Senate Reports: No. 91-1139 accompanying S. 3678 (Comm. on Banking and Currency)

Congressional Record, Vol. 116 (1970)

May 25, considered and passed House.

Sept. 18, considered and passed Senate, amended.

Oct. 9, Senate agreed to conference report.

Oct. 13, House agreed to conference report.

Enactment: Public Law No. 91-508 (October 26, 1970):

Amendments: Public Law Nos. 95-473 (October 17, 1978)

95-598 (November 6, 1978)

98-443 (October 4, 1984)

101-73 (August 9, 1989)

102-242 (December 19, 1991)

102-537 (October 27, 1992)

102-550 (October 28, 1992)

103-325 (September 23, 1994)

104-88 (December 29, 1995)

104-93 (January 6, 1996)

104-193 (August 22, 1996)

104-208 (September 30, 1996)

105-107 (November 20, 1997)

105-347 (November 2, 1998)

106-102 (November 12, 1999)

107-56 (October 26, 2001)

108-159 (December 4, 2003)

THE FAIR DEBT COLLECTION PRACTICES ACT

As amended by Pub. L. 109-351, §§ 801-02, 120 Stat. 1966 (2006)

As a public service, the staff of the Federal Trade Commission (FTC) has prepared the following complete text of the Fair Debt Collection Practices Act (FDCPA), 15 U.S.C. §§ 1692-1692p.

Please note that the format of the text differs in minor ways from the U.S. Code and West's U.S. Code Annotated. For example, this version uses FDCPA section numbers in the headings. In addition, the relevant U.S. Code citation is included with each section heading. Although the staff has made every effort to transcribe the statutory material accurately, this compendium is intended as a convenience for the public and not a substitute for the text in the U.S. Code.

Table of Contents

§ 813 Civil liability

§ 814 Administrative enforcement

§ 815 Reports to Congress by the Commission

§ 816 Relation to State laws

§ 817 Exemption for State regulation

§ 818 Exception for certain bad check enforcement programs operated by private entities

§ 819 Effective date

§ 801. Short Title

This title may be cited as the "Fair Debt Collection Practices Act."

§ 802. Congressional findings and declaration of purpose

(a) There is abundant evidence of the use of abusive, deceptive, and unfair debt collection practices by many debt collectors. Abusive debt collection practices contribute to the number of personal bankruptcies, to marital instability, to the loss of jobs, and to invasions of individual privacy.

(b) Existing laws and procedures for redressing these injuries are inadequate to protect consumers.

(c) Means other than misrepresentation or other abusive debt collection practices are available for the effective collection of debts.

(d) Abusive debt collection practices are carried on to a substantial extent in interstate commerce and through means and instrumentalities of such commerce. Even where abusive debt collection practices are purely intrastate in character, they nevertheless directly affect interstate commerce.

(e) It is the purpose of this title to eliminate abusive debt collection practices by debt collectors, to insure that those debt collectors who refrain from using abusive debt collection practices are not competitively disadvantaged, and to promote consistent State action to protect consumers against debt collection abuses.

§ 803. Definitions

As used in this title—

(1) The term "Commission" means the Federal Trade Commission.

(2) The term "communication" means the conveying of information regarding a debt directly or indirectly to any person through any medium.

(3) The term "consumer" means any natural person obligated or allegedly obligated to pay any debt.

(4) The term "creditor" means any person who offers or extends credit creating a debt or to whom a debt is owed, but such term does not include any person to the extent that he receives an assignment or transfer of a debt in default solely for the purpose of facilitating collection of such debt for another.

(5) The term "debt" means any obligation or alleged obligation of a consumer to pay money arising out of a transaction in which the money, property, insurance or services which are the subject of the transaction are primarily for personal, family, or household purposes, whether or not such obligation has been reduced to judgment.

(6) The term "debt collector" means any person who uses any instrumentality of interstate commerce or the mails in any business the principal purpose of which is the collection of any debts, or who regularly collects or attempts to collect, directly or indirectly, debts owed or due or asserted to be owed or due another. Notwithstanding the exclusion provided by clause (F) of the last sentence of this paragraph, the term includes any creditor who, in the process of collecting his own debts, uses any name other than his own which would indicate that a third person is collecting or attempting to collect such debts. For the purpose of section 808(6), such term also includes any person who uses any instrumentality of interstate commerce or the mails in any business the principal purpose of which is the enforcement of security interests. The term does not include—

(A) any officer or employee of a creditor while, in the name of the creditor, collecting debts for such creditor;

(B) any person while acting as a debt collector for another person, both of whom are related by common ownership or affiliated by corporate control, if the person acting as a debt collector does so only for persons to whom it is so related or affiliated and if the principal business of such person is not the collection of debts;

(C) any officer or employee of the United States or any State to the extent that collecting or attempting to collect any debt is in the performance of his official duties;

(D) any person while serving or attempting to serve legal process on any other person in connection with the judicial enforcement of any debt;

(E) any nonprofit organization which, at the request of consumers, performs bona fide consumer credit counseling and assists consumers in the liquidation of their debts by receiving payments from such consumers and distributing such amounts to creditors; and

(F) any person collecting or attempting to collect any debt owed or due or asserted to be owed or due another to the extent such activity

(i) is incidental to a bona fide fiduciary obligation or a bona fide escrow arrangement;

(ii) concerns a debt which was originated by such person;

(iii) concerns a debt which was not in default at the time it was obtained by such person; or

(iv) concerns a debt obtained by such person as a secured party in a commercial credit transaction involving the creditor.

(7) The term "location information" means a consumer's place of abode and his telephone number at such place, or his place of employment.

(8) The term "State" means any State, territory, or possession of the United States, the District of Columbia, the Commonwealth of Puerto Rico, or any political subdivision of any of the foregoing.

§ 804. Acquisition of location information

Any debt collector communicating with any person other than the consumer for the purpose of acquiring location information about the consumer shall—

(1) identify himself, state that he is confirming or correcting location information concerning the consumer, and, only if expressly requested, identify his employer;

(2) not state that such consumer owes any debt;

(3) not communicate with any such person more than once unless requested to do so by such person or unless the debt collector reasonably believes that the earlier response of such person is erroneous or incomplete and that such person now has correct or complete location information;

(4) not communicate by post card;

(5) not use any language or symbol on any envelope or in the contents of any communication effected by the mails or telegram that indicates that the debt collector is in the debt collection business or that the communication relates to the collection of a debt; and

(6) after the debt collector knows the consumer is represented by an attorney with regard to the subject debt and has knowledge of, or can readily ascertain, such attorney's name and address, not communicate with any person other than that attorney, unless the attorney fails to respond within a reasonable period of time to the communication from the debt collector.

§ 805. Communication in connection with debt collection

(a) COMMUNICATION WITH THE CONSUMER GENER-ALLY. Without the prior consent of the consumer given directly to the debt collector or the express permission of a court of competent jurisdiction, a debt collector may not communicate with a consumer in connection with the collection of any debt—

(1) at any unusual time or place or a time or place known or which should be known to be inconvenient to the consumer. In the absence of knowledge of circumstances to the contrary, a debt collector shall assume that the convenient time for

communicating with a consumer is after 8 o'clock antimeridian and before 9 o'clock postmeridian, local time at the consumer's location;

(2) if the debt collector knows the consumer is represented by an attorney with respect to such debt and has knowledge of, or can readily ascertain, such attorney's name and address, unless the attorney fails to respond within a reasonable period of time to a communication from the debt collector or unless the attorney consents to direct communication with the consumer; or

(3) at the consumer's place of employment if the debt collector knows or has reason to know that the consumer's employer prohibits the consumer from receiving such communication.

(b) COMMUNICATION WITH THIRD PARTIES. Except as provided in section 804, without the prior consent of the consumer given directly to the debt collector, or the express permission of a court of competent jurisdiction, or as reasonably necessary to effectuate a postjudgment judicial remedy, a debt collector may not communicate, in connection with the collection of any debt, with any person other than a consumer, his attorney, a consumer reporting agency if otherwise permitted by law, the creditor, the attorney of the creditor, or the attorney of the debt collector.

(c) CEASING COMMUNICATION. If a consumer notifies a debt collector in writing that the consumer refuses to pay a debt or that the consumer wishes the debt collector to cease further communication with the consumer, the debt collector shall not communicate further with the consumer with respect to such debt, except—

(1) to advise the consumer that the debt collector's further efforts are being terminated;

(2) to notify the consumer that the debt collector or creditor may invoke specified remedies which are ordinarily invoked by such debt collector or creditor; or

(3) where applicable, to notify the consumer that the debt collector or creditor intends to invoke a specified remedy.

If such notice from the consumer is made by mail, notification shall be complete upon receipt.

(d) For the purpose of this section, the term "consumer" includes the consumer's spouse, parent (if the consumer is a minor), guardian, executor, or administrator.

§ 806. Harassment or abuse

A debt collector may not engage in any conduct the natural consequence of which is to harass, oppress, or abuse any person in connection with the collection of a debt. Without limiting the general application of the foregoing, the following conduct is a violation of this section:

(1) The use or threat of use of violence or other criminal means to harm the physical person, reputation, or property of any person.

(2) The use of obscene or profane language or language the natural consequence of which is to abuse the hearer or reader.

(3) The publication of a list of consumers who allegedly refuse to pay debts, except to a consumer reporting agency or to persons meeting the requirements of section 603(f) or 604(3)[1] of this Act.

(4) The advertisement for sale of any debt to coerce payment of the debt.

(5) Causing a telephone to ring or engaging any person in telephone conversation repeatedly or continuously with intent to annoy, abuse, or harass any person at the called number.

(6) Except as provided in section 804, the placement of telephone calls without meaningful disclosure of the caller's identity.

1. Section 604(3) has been renumbered as Section 604(a)(3).

§ 807. False or misleading representations

A debt collector may not use any false, deceptive, or misleading representation or means in connection with the collection of any debt.

Without limiting the general application of the foregoing, the following conduct is a violation of this section:

(1) The false representation or implication that the debt collector is vouched for, bonded by, or affiliated with the United States or any State, including the use of any badge, uniform, or facsimile thereof.

(2) The false representation of—

(A) the character, amount, or legal status of any debt; or

(B) any services rendered or compensation which may be lawfully received by any debt collector for the collection of a debt.

(3) The false representation or implication that any individual is an attorney or that any communication is from an attorney.

(4) The representation or implication that nonpayment of any debt will result in the arrest or imprisonment of any person or the seizure, garnishment, attachment, or sale of any property or wages of any person unless such action is lawful and the debt collector or creditor intends to take such action.

(5) The threat to take any action that cannot legally be taken or that is not intended to be taken.

(6) The false representation or implication that a sale, referral, or other transfer of any interest in a debt shall cause the consumer to—

(A) lose any claim or defense to payment of the debt; or

(B) become subject to any practice prohibited by this title.

(7) The false representation or implication that the consumer committed any crime or other conduct in order to disgrace the consumer.

(8) Communicating or threatening to communicate to any person credit information which is known or which should be known to be false, including the failure to communicate that a disputed debt is disputed.

(9) The use or distribution of any written communication which simulates or is falsely represented to be a document authorized, issued, or approved by any court, official, or agency of the United

States or any State, or which creates a false impression as to its source, authorization, or approval.

(10) The use of any false representation or deceptive means to collect or attempt to collect any debt or to obtain information concerning a consumer.

(11) The failure to disclose in the initial written communication with the consumer and, in addition, if the initial communication with the consumer is oral, in that initial oral communication, that the debt collector is attempting to collect a debt and that any information obtained will be used for that purpose, and the failure to disclose in subsequent communications that the communication is from a debt collector, except that this paragraph shall not apply to a formal pleading made in connection with a legal action.

(12) The false representation or implication that accounts have been turned over to innocent purchasers for value.

(13) The false representation or implication that documents are legal process.

(14) The use of any business, company, or organization name other than the true name of the debt collector's business, company, or organization.

(15) The false representation or implication that documents are not legal process forms or do not require action by the consumer.

(16) The false representation or implication that a debt collector operates or is employed by a consumer reporting agency as defined by section 603(f) of this Act.

§ 808. Unfair practices

A debt collector may not use unfair or unconscionable means to collect or attempt to collect any debt. Without limiting the general application of the foregoing, the following conduct is a violation of this section:

(1) The collection of any amount (including any interest, fee, charge, or expense incidental to the principal obligation) unless such amount is expressly authorized by the agreement creating the debt

or permitted by law.

(2) The acceptance by a debt collector from any person of a check or other payment instrument postdated by more than five days unless such person is notified in writing of the debt collector's intent to deposit such check or instrument not more than ten nor less than three business days prior to such deposit.

(3) The solicitation by a debt collector of any postdated check or other postdated payment instrument for the purpose of threatening or instituting criminal prosecution.

(4) Depositing or threatening to deposit any postdated check or other postdated payment instrument prior to the date on such check or instrument.

(5) Causing charges to be made to any person for communications by concealment of the true propose of the communication. Such charges include, but are not limited to, collect telephone calls and telegram fees.

(6) Taking or threatening to take any nonjudicial action to effect dispossession or disablement of property if—

(A) there is no present right to possession of the property claimed as collateral through an enforceable security interest;

(B) there is no present intention to take possession of the property; or

(C) the property is exempt by law from such dispossession or disablement.

(7) Communicating with a consumer regarding a debt by post card.

(8) Using any language or symbol, other than the debt collector's address, on any envelope when communicating with a consumer by use of the mails or by telegram, except that a debt collector may use his business name if such name does not indicate that he is in the debt collection business.

§ 809. Validation of debts

(a) Within five days after the initial communication with a consumer in connection with the collection of any debt, a debt collector shall, unless the following information is contained in the initial communication or the consumer has paid the debt, send the consumer a written notice containing—

(1) the amount of the debt;

(2) the name of the creditor to whom the debt is owed;

(3) a statement that unless the consumer, within thirty days after receipt of the notice, disputes the validity of the debt, or any portion thereof, the debt will be assumed to be valid by the debt collector;

(4) a statement that if the consumer notifies the debt collector in writing within the thirty-day period that the debt, or any portion thereof, is disputed, the debt collector will obtain verification of the debt or a copy of a judgment against the consumer and a copy of such verification or judgment will be mailed to the consumer by the debt collector; and

(5) a statement that, upon the consumer's written request within the thirty-day period, the debt collector will provide the consumer with the name and address of the original creditor, if different from the current creditor.

(b) If the consumer notifies the debt collector in writing within the thirty-day period described in subsection (a) that the debt, or any portion thereof, is disputed, or that the consumer requests the name and address of the original creditor, the debt collector shall cease collection of the debt, or any disputed portion thereof, until the debt collector obtains verification of the debt or any copy of a judgment, or the name and address of the original creditor, and a copy of such verification or judgment, or name and address of the original creditor, is mailed to the consumer by the debt collector. Collection activities and communications that do not otherwise violate this title may continue during the 30-day period referred to in subsection (a) unless the consumer has notified the debt collector in writing that the debt, or any portion of the debt, is disputed or that the consumer requests the name and address of the original creditor. Any collection activities and communication during the 30-day period may not overshadow or be inconsistent with the disclosure of the consumer's right to dispute the debt or request the name and address of the original creditor.

(c) The failure of a consumer to dispute the validity of a debt under this section may not be construed by any court as an admission of liability by the consumer.

(d) A communication in the form of a formal pleading in a civil action shall not be treated as an initial communication for purposes of subsection (a).

(e) The sending or delivery of any form or notice which does not relate to the collection of a debt and is expressly required by the Internal Revenue Code of 1986, title V of Gramm-Leach-Bliley Act, or any provision of Federal or State law relating to notice of data security breach or privacy, or any regulation prescribed under any such provision of law, shall not be treated as an initial communication in connection with debt collection for purposes of this section.

§ 810. Multiple debts

If any consumer owes multiple debts and makes any single payment to any debt collector with respect to such debts, such debt collector may not apply such payment to any debt which is disputed by the consumer and, where applicable, shall apply such payment in accordance with the consumer's directions.

§ 811. Legal actions by debt collectors

(a) Any debt collector who brings any legal action on a debt against any consumer shall—

(1) in the case of an action to enforce an interest in real property securing the consumer's obligation, bring such action only in a judicial district or similar legal entity in which such real property is located; or

(2) in the case of an action not described in paragraph (1), bring such action only in the judicial district or similar legal entity—

(A) in which such consumer signed the contract sued upon; or

(B) in which such consumer resides at the commencement of the action.

(b) Nothing in this title shall be construed to authorize the bringing of legal actions by debt collectors.

§ 812. Furnishing certain deceptive forms

(a) It is unlawful to design, compile, and furnish any form knowing that such form would be used to create the false belief in a consumer that a person other than the creditor of such consumer is participating in the collection of or in an attempt to collect a debt such consumer allegedly owes such creditor, when in fact such person is not so participating.

(b) Any person who violates this section shall be liable to the same extent and in the same manner as a debt collector is liable under section 813 for failure to comply with a provision of this title.

§ 813. Civil liability

(a) Except as otherwise provided by this section, any debt collector who fails to comply with any provision of this title with respect to any person is liable to such person in an amount equal to the sum of—

   (1) any actual damage sustained by such person as a result of such failure;

   (2) (A) in the case of any action by an individual, such additional damages as the court may allow, but not exceeding $1,000; or

   (B) in the case of a class action,

       (i) such amount for each named plaintiff as could be recovered under subparagraph (A), and

       (ii) such amount as the court may allow for all other class members, without regard to a minimum individual recovery, not to exceed the lesser of $500,000 or 1 per centum of the net worth of the debt collector; and

   (3) in the case of any successful action to enforce the foregoing liability, the costs of the action, together with a reasonable attorney's fee as determined by the court. On a finding by the court that an action under this section was brought in bad faith and for the purpose of harassment, the court

may award to the defendant attorney's fees reasonable in relation to the work expended and costs.

(b) In determining the amount of liability in any action under subsection (a), the court shall consider, among other relevant factors—

(1) in any individual action under subsection (a)(2)(A), the frequency and persistence of noncompliance by the debt collector, the nature of such noncompliance, and the extent to which such noncompliance was intentional; or

(2) in any class action under subsection (a)(2)(B), the frequency and persistence of noncompliance by the debt collector, the nature of such noncompliance, the resources of the debt collector, the number of persons adversely affected, and the extent to which the debt collector's noncompliance was intentional.

(c) A debt collector may not be held liable in any action brought under this title if the debt collector shows by a preponderance of evidence that the violation was not intentional and resulted from a bona fide error notwithstanding the maintenance of procedures reasonably adapted to avoid any such error.

(d) An action to enforce any liability created by this title may be brought in any appropriate United States district court without regard to the amount in controversy, or in any other court of competent jurisdiction, within one year from the date on which the violation occurs.

(e) No provision of this section imposing any liability shall apply to any act done or omitted in good faith in conformity with any advisory opinion of the Commission, notwithstanding that after such act or omission has occurred, such opinion is amended, rescinded, or determined by judicial· or other authority to be invalid for any reason.

§ 814. Administrative enforcement

(a) Compliance with this title shall be enforced by the Commission, except to the extent that enforcement of the requirements imposed under this title is specifically committed to another agency under subsection (b). For purpose of the exercise by the Commission of its functions and powers under the Federal Trade Commission

Act, a violation of this title shall be deemed an unfair or deceptive act or practice in violation of that Act. All of the functions and powers of the Commission under the Federal Trade Commission Act are available to the Commission to enforce compliance by any person with this title, irrespective of whether that person is engaged in commerce or meets any other jurisdictional tests in the Federal Trade Commission Act, including the power to enforce the provisions of this title in the same manner as if the violation had been a violation of a Federal Trade Commission trade regulation rule.

(b) Compliance with any requirements imposed under this title shall be enforced under—

(1) section 8 of the Federal Deposit Insurance Act, in the case of—

    (A) national banks, and Federal branches and Federal agencies of foreign banks, by the Office of the Comptroller of the Currency;

    (B) member banks of the Federal Reserve System (other than national banks), branches and agencies of foreign banks (other than Federal branches, Federal agencies, and insured State branches of foreign banks), commercial lending companies owned or controlled by foreign banks, and organizations operating under section 25 or 25(a) of the Federal Reserve Act, by the Board of Governors of the Federal Reserve System; and

    (C) banks insured by the Federal Deposit Insurance Corporation (other than members of the Federal Reserve System) and insured State branches of foreign banks, by the Board of Directors of the Federal Deposit Insurance Corporation;

(2) section 8 of the Federal Deposit Insurance Act, by the Director of the Office of Thrift Supervision, in the case of a savings association the deposits of which are insured by the Federal Deposit Insurance Corporation;

(3) the Federal Credit Union Act, by the Administrator of the National Credit Union Administration with respect to any Federal credit union;

(4) the Acts to regulate commerce, by the Secretary of Transportation,

with respect to all carriers subject to the jurisdiction of the Surface Transportation Board;

(5) the Federal Aviation Act of 1958, by the Secretary of Transportation with respect to any air carrier or any foreign air carrier subject to that Act; and

(6) the Packers and Stockyards Act, 1921 (except as provided in section 406 of that Act), by the Secretary of Agriculture with respect to any activities subject to that Act.

The terms used in paragraph (1) that are not defined in this title or otherwise defined in section 3(s) of the Federal Deposit Insurance Act (12 U.S.C. 1813(s)) shall have the meaning given to them in section 1(b) of the International Banking Act of 1978 (12 U.S.C. 3101).

(c) For the purpose of the exercise by any agency referred to in subsection (b) of its powers under any Act referred to in that subsection, a violation of any requirement imposed under this title shall be deemed to be a violation of a requirement imposed under that Act. In addition to its powers under any provision of law specifically referred to in subsection (b), each of the agencies referred to in that subsection may exercise, for the purpose of enforcing compliance with any requirement imposed under this title any other authority conferred on it by law, except as provided in subsection (d).

(d) Neither the Commission nor any other agency referred to in subsection (b) may promulgate trade regulation rules or other regulations with respect to the collection of debts by debt collectors as defined in this title.

§ 815. Reports to Congress by the Commission

(a) Not later than one year after the effective date of this title and at one-year intervals thereafter, the Commission shall make reports to the Congress concerning the administration of its functions under this title, including such recommendations as the Commission deems necessary or appropriate. In addition, each report of the Commission shall include its assessment of the extent to which compliance with this title is being achieved and a summary of the enforcement actions taken by the Commission under section 814 of this title.

(b) In the exercise of its functions under this title, the Commission may obtain upon request the views of any other Federal agency which exercises enforcement functions under section 814 of this title.

§ 816. Relation to State laws

This title does not annul, alter, or affect, or exempt any person subject to the provisions of this title from complying with the laws of any State with respect to debt collection practices, except to the extent that those laws are inconsistent with any provision of this title, and then only to the extent of the inconsistency. For purposes of this section, a State law is not inconsistent with this title if the protection such law affords any consumer is greater than the protection provided by this title.

§ 817. Exemption for State regulation

The Commission shall by regulation exempt from the requirements of this title any class of debt collection practices within any State if the Commission determines that under the law of that State that class of debt collection practices is subject to requirements substantially similar to those imposed by this title, and that there is adequate provision for enforcement.

§ 818. Exception for certain bad check enforcement programs operated by private entities

(a) In General.—

(1) TREATMENT OF CERTAIN PRIVATE ENTITIES.— Subject to paragraph (2), a private entity shall be excluded from the definition of a debt collector, pursuant to the exception provided in section 803(6), with respect to the operation by the entity of a program described in paragraph (2)(A) under a contract described in paragraph (2)(B).

(2) CONDITIONS OF APPLICABILITY.—Paragraph (1) shall apply if—

(A) a State or district attorney establishes, within the jurisdiction of such State or district attorney and with respect to alleged bad check violations that do not involve a check described in subsection (b), a pretrial diversion program for alleged bad check offenders who agree to participate voluntarily in such program to avoid criminal prosecution;

(B) a private entity, that is subject to an administrative support services contract with a State or district attorney and operates under the direction, supervision, and control of such State or district attorney, operates the pretrial diversion program described in subparagraph (A); and

(C) in the course of performing duties delegated to it by a State or district attorney under the contract, the private entity referred to in subparagraph (B)—

(i) complies with the penal laws of the State;

(ii) conforms with the terms of the contract and directives of the State or district attorney;

(iii) does not exercise independent prosecutorial discretion;

(iv) contacts any alleged offender referred to in subparagraph (A) for purposes of participating in a program referred to in such paragraph—

(I) only as a result of any determination by the State or district attorney that probable cause of a bad check violation under State penal law exists, and that contact with the alleged offender for purposes of participation in the program is appropriate; and

(II) the alleged offender has failed to pay the bad check after demand for payment, pursuant to State law, is made for payment of the check amount;

(v) includes as part of an initial written communication with an alleged offender a clear and conspicuous statement that—

(I) the alleged offender may dispute the validity of any alleged bad check violation;

(II) where the alleged offender knows, or has reasonable cause to believe, that the alleged bad check violation is the result of theft or forgery of the check, identity theft, other fraud that is not the result of the conduct of the alleged offender, the alleged offender may file a crime report with the appropriate law enforcement agency; and

(III) if the alleged offender notifies the private entity or the district attorney in writing, not later than 30 days after being contacted for the first time pursuant to clause (iv), that there is a dispute pursuant to this subsection, before further restitution efforts are pursued, the district attorney or an employee of the district attorney authorized to make such a determination makes a determination that there is probable cause to believe that a crime has been committed; and

(vi) charges only fees in connection with services under the contract that have been authorized by the contract with the State or district attorney.

(b) Certain Checks Excluded.—A check is described in this subsection if the check involves, or is subsequently found to involve—

(1) a postdated check presented in connection with a payday loan, or other similar transaction, where the payee of the check knew that the issuer had insufficient funds at the time the check was made, drawn, or delivered;

(2) a stop payment order where the issuer acted in good faith and with reasonable cause in stopping payment on the check;

(3) a check dishonored because of an adjustment to the issuer's account by the financial institution holding such account without providing notice to the person at the time the check was made, drawn, or delivered;

(4) a check for partial payment of a debt where the payee had previously accepted partial payment for such debt;

(5) a check issued by a person who was not competent, or was not of legal age, to enter into a legal contractual obligation at the time the check was made, drawn, or delivered; or

(6) a check issued to pay an obligation arising from a transaction that was illegal in the jurisdiction of the State or district attorney at the time the check was made, drawn, or delivered.

(c) Definitions.—For purposes of this section, the following definitions shall apply:

(1) STATE OR DISTRICT ATTORNEY.—The term "State or district attorney" means the chief elected or appointed prosecuting attorney in a district, county (as defined in section 2 of title 1, United States Code), municipality, or comparable jurisdiction, including State attorneys general who act as chief elected or appointed prosecuting attorneys in a district, county (as so defined), municipality or comparable jurisdiction, who may be referred to by a variety of titles such as district attorneys, prosecuting attorneys, commonwealth's attorneys, solicitors, county attorneys, and state's attorneys, and who are responsible for the prosecution of State crimes and violations of jurisdiction-specific local ordinances.

(2) CHECK.—The term "check" has the same meaning as in section 3(6) of the Check Clearing for the 21st Century Act.

(3) BAD CHECK VIOLATION.—The term "bad check violation" means a violation of the applicable State criminal law relating to the writing of dishonored checks.

§ 819. Effective date

This title takes effect upon the expiration of six months after the date of its enactment, but section 809 shall apply only with respect to debts for which the initial attempt to collect occurs after such effective date.

Legislative History

House Report: No. 95-131 (Comm. on Banking, Finance, and Urban Affairs)

Senate Report: No. 95-382 (Comm. on Banking, Housing and Urban Affairs)

Congressional Record, Vol. 123 (1977)

April 4, House considered and passed H.R. 5294.

Aug. 5, Senate considered and passed amended version of H.R. 5294.

Sept. 8, House considered and passed Senate version.

Enactment: Public Law 95-109 (Sept. 20, 1977)

Amendments: Public Law Nos.

99-361 (July 9, 1986)

101-73 (Aug. 9, 1989)

102-242 (Dec. 19, 1991)

102-550 (Oct. 28, 1992)

104-88 (Dec. 29, 1995)

104-208 (Sept. 30, 1996)

109-351 (Oct. 13, 2006)23

Revised January 2009 for the consumer 1-877-FTC-HELP, ftc.gov Federal Trade Commission

Find consumer credit lawyers: www.naca.net/

Statute of limitations for all states: www.carreonandassociates.com/articles/sol.htm

Free credit report website: www.annualcreditreport.com/cra/index.jsp

Best credit card deals: www.creditcards.com/

Journey to Wealth Inc.: www.Journeytowealth.net

Journey to Wealth Products

Order these forms at www.Journeytowealth.net:

Debt settlement letters: These letters can help you remove negative listings from your credit report.

Debt validation letters: These letters are the ultimate weapon to use against collection agencies. Leverage the protection of the FDCPA, eliminate your debt, and remove the negative trade line from your credit report.

Credit repair letters: These letters can help remove negative listings, such as charge-offs, tax liens, and bankruptcy.

The Guide to Starting a Home-Based Credit Repair Business: This guide shows you how to earn money repairing other people's credit. It discusses how to set up, promote, and operate your credit repair business.

How to Create Your Own Real Estate Fortune: This guide shows you how to leverage creative financing ideas to find investment opportunities in real estate.

Visit this web page for upcoming seminars, webinars, and workshops on credit repair, earning extra income with your own credit repair business, and leveraging your good credit into wealth: www.Journeytowealth.net.

www.ingramcontent.com/pod-product-compliance
Lightning Source LLC
Chambersburg PA
CBHW032000170526
45157CB00002B/474